PRAISE FOR *LEAN ON ME*

My favorite stories are honest and warm, full of courage and missteps and trying again, full of love and friendship and walking through the mess of it all together. And this, certainly, is one of those stories.

—SHAUNA NIEQUIST, AUTHOR OF *BREAD AND WINE*

Anne Miller plunges into the many complexities found within deep and vulnerable relationships, by allowing us into her own. With every page, she deftly rotates this written prism, and in doing so, illuminates something new—not just about her experiences, fears, and desires, but also about my own. Tangible and personal, heartbreaking and hopeful, *Lean On Me* is a rare gift.

—JOSH JAMES RIEBOCK, AUTHOR OF *HEROES AND MONSTERS* AND *MY GENERATION*

On behalf of community-challenged people everywhere, I offer a sincere thank you to Anne Marie Miller—for writing her story in a way that vulnerably *shows* what it means to live in community when it may have been easier for her to try to tell us how to do it. She writes not as an expert but as a fellow journeyer. If you're longing to live your life with others but aren't quite sure what that looks like, Anne's beautiful story will be a kind companion, always pointing towards hope.

—EMILY P. FREEMAN, AUTHOR OF *A MILLION LITTLE WAYS*

Anne Miller writes about subjects that no one else has the courage to address. She says what the rest of us are thinking but can't quite bring ourselves to say. But it's not the affront you'd imagine it would be. Like a warm novel, her writing draws us in, stirs us in the deepest places, and brings out our very best. *Lean On Me* is no exception to her growing catalog of extraordinary writing.

—BEN ARMENT, CREATOR OF STORY AND AUTHOR OF *DREAM YEAR*

We live in a world that's more connected than ever before and yet research continues to show we've never been lonelier. How do we find community—real, heart-healing, love-you-as-you-are community? That's the question Anne Marie Miller explores on these pages. Through her personal story and spiritual insights she shares how we can truly discover what it means to love one another. And why doing so changes everything.

—HOLLEY GERTH, BEST-SELLING AUTHOR OF *YOU'RE ALREADY AMAZING*

Another record of someone's story? Yes, but this one is unique. Engagingly well written, but far more importantly, Anne's story is a disturbingly searching, deeply convicting, and delightfully arousing call to community, the kind that only Jesus makes possible. Read it and you'll want to relate as perhaps you've never related before, with both vulnerability and commitment. Leave safe relating behind, and connect with healing power.

—LARRY CRABB, BEST-SELLING AUTHOR OF *CONNECTING*

I have always loved how the book of James chapter 3 describes community as "the hard work of getting along." In Anne's book we get a firsthand, living, breathing example of what that looks like as she opens up her story and her deliberate pursuit of community to us. Choosing to stay in community when running away seemed so much easier is the hard choice that Anne unpacks for us, giving us the courage to choose it for ourselves. And offering concrete hope and examples for anyone who feels lost in the crowd and hungry for community.

—LISA-JO BAKER, BEST-SELLING AUTHOR OF *SURPRISED BY MOTHERHOOD* AND COMMUNITY MANAGER FOR (IN)COURAGE

Lean On Me has touched that place in me that longs for community, guiding me in the how, sparking hope for my future. It is a book for the introvert and extrovert, those who have committed to community and those who have run from it. Bravo on this book, Anne Marie

Miller. You are elegant and honest in the pages. I carry your wise words with me.

—LISA WHITTLE, SPEAKER AND AUTHOR OF *{W}HOLE* AND *I WANT GOD*

There's a common thread woven in and out of most all of our lives—seasons of heartbreak. Whether it's divorce, a friendship breakup, or another one of those split-open times of vulnerable hurt and rejection, we desperately need a friend to give us hope-filled reassurances. That's my friend, Anne Marie Miller, and her book *Lean On Me*. Reading this gut-honest book will be like cold water to your parched soul. She's tender, brilliant, and persevering. Get this book!

—LYSA TERKEURST, *NEW YORK TIMES* BEST-SELLING AUTHOR OF *UNGLUED* AND PRESIDENT OF PROVERBS 31 MINISTRIES

Anne Miller has done the hard work of living vulnerably in front of her community and, in the end, being all the better for it. *Lean On Me* is an honest and moving memoir of a life season that forever marked her and her people and drew all closer to Jesus. There is much to be gained in wisdom and heart as you read this book.

—ANNIE F. DOWNS, AUTHOR OF *LET'S ALL BE BRAVE*

Lean On Me

*Finding Intentional, Vulnerable,
and Consistent Community*

ANNE MARIE MILLER

W PUBLISHING GROUP

AN IMPRINT OF THOMAS NELSON

© 2014 by Anne Marie Miller

All rights reserved. No portion of this book may be reproduced, stored in a retrieval system, or transmitted in any form or by any means—electronic, mechanical, photocopy, recording, scanning, or other—except for brief quotations in critical reviews or articles, without the prior written permission of the publisher.

Published in Nashville, Tennessee, by W Publishing, an imprint of Thomas Nelson.

Thomas Nelson, Inc. titles may be purchased in bulk for educational, business, fund-raising, or sales promotional use. For information, please e-mail SpecialMarkets@ ThomasNelson.com.

Unless otherwise noted, Scripture quotations are from The Holy Bible, New International Version®, NIV®. Copyright ©1973, 1978, 1984 by Biblica, Inc.™ Used by permission of Zondervan. All rights reserved worldwide. www.zondervan.com.

Scripture quotations marked NLT are from Holy Bible, New Living Translation. © 1996. Used by permission of Tyndale House Publishers, Inc., Wheaton, Illinois 60189. All rights reserved.

Scripture quotations marked ESV are from THE ENGLISH STANDARD VERSION. © 2001 by Crossway Bibles, a division of Good News Publishers.

Scripture quotations marked The Voice are taken from The Voice. © 2012 Ecclesia Bible Society. Used by permission. All rights reserved.

In order to respect the privacy of those who were unable to be contacted, names and irrelevant details have been changed. Sometimes one character in this book is a composite of many characters in my life. I appreciate the life and light each of them brought, even if they weren't uniquely identified.

Library of Congress Control Number: 2014942537

ISBN 978-0-8499-4600-4

Printed in the United States of America

14 15 16 17 18 RRD 6 5 4 3 2 1

For Jay Williams—who lived and died
loving others with courage and grace

It is my prayer that the Holy Spirit guides and directs you as you read through these pages. May you know because of the unity of believers through Christ across all time and space, you are never alone as you venture through your sleeping and your waking.

Peace of Christ, Anne Marie Miller

CONTENTS

....

part 1

·············

The Makeup of Community

That is part of the beauty of all literature. You discover that your longings are universal longings, that you're not lonely and isolated from anyone. You belong.

—F. SCOTT FITZGERALD

*C*ommunity.

It's a word we encounter from the pulpits of our churches to the blogs we read. We desire rich relationships where we can live without masks and love without fear. Places where we are truly known and because of our brokenness—not in spite of it—we are cherished. Our souls are laced with this need; it's implanted into our very DNA. Like the famous song says, "We all need somebody to lean on."

Yet oftentimes, we feel alone, or in many instances, lonely.

Even though we need people in the small moments of our lives, sometimes it takes a catastrophic event to confront us with the reality of where we stand in our relationship with others and our interdependency with them.

In any case, that is my story. *This . . .* is my story. And in it, I hope you can find, as F. Scott Fitzgerald said, "You're not lonely and isolated from anyone. You belong."

1

CREATED FOR BELONGING

Perhaps home is not a place but simply
an irrevocable condition.

—JAMES BALDWIN, *GIOVANNI'S ROOM*

an you feel it?

Buried into the molecules and electricity that cause our hearts to beat, lives and breathes a longing we can only attempt to describe. It is not inert; it moves and grows and feels pain and rejoices, and it can do all of these things in chorus with little effort on our part.

This desire demands our attention, much like an infant crying out for his mother. There are no coherent words and no formed questions, just a cry that can be best interpreted as, *Please be with me. Nourish me. Warm me. Embrace me. Love me. See me.*

However loud this cry, a duality also exists, just as hidden and puzzling. We desperately want to belong, yet at the same time we yearn for independence. We want to prove to ourselves and those around us we can survive on our own. That we are not dependent. We are free. *To rely on someone else is weakness*, this conflicting voice utters. The ears of our spirits listen.

These two voices are innate. The first humans lost their native divine dependence when they consumed knowledge from a tree. It is a daily struggle and a daily surrender to allow ourselves the freedom to wrestle with our holy need for interdependence upon each other in the body of Christ.

....

Where do I belong?

I never knew how to answer that question. In thirty-four years of life, I've lived all over the United States, up and down Interstate 35 from Dallas to Kansas City, with a short six-month stop in Oklahoma along the way. I went north to Michigan, and over to the plains of western Illinois. Further west to Los Angeles. East to Nashville.

When I was a child, my father, a Baptist pastor, was called to a new church every couple of years or so, and the routine was the same each time: our family of four crowded into the cab of a barely street-legal yellow moving truck he paid for in cash, and away we went down the boiling Texas interstate to whatever destination was next in our future. We rolled the truck windows all the way down, which gave the impression of having air-conditioning but in reality only allowed in the hot, gritty air. My scrawny legs stuck to the grey vinyl seats as Neil Diamond sang to us through the truck's speakers on the journey to our new home. The tape player was the one part on the moving truck that always functioned without fail.

When I was five years old, our house and the church next door were the only signs of human life for miles in a patchwork of four Texas farms. The nearest neighbor was a fifteen-minute drive on dirt roads built above irrigation canals, unless one walked across the five-hundred-acre plot behind our house. When we moved in a month or two before harvest time, it was a fortress of corn twice as tall as me, hiding the habitat around us. But after the combines cleared the land, I could see straight across the empty red earth to my friend Stephanie's house.

Rattlesnakes, bobcats, and a feral mismatch of other not-so-kind desert creatures brought out the protective side in my parents. My younger brother and I were only allowed to play in the dirt parking lot of the church or near the front porch if we went outside. After one particular disagreement with my parents, I decided I was going to run away. I was emancipating myself. No longer would I give in to their demands and unfair chores like scrubbing the green beans and carrots we grew in our garden.

I carefully packed all my valuables in an aluminum Sesame Street lunch box and went to the porch. I waited. With my mom's watchful eye following my every move, I sat in the dirt under the honeysuckle vines that took over the black metal railing. I hid in its shadow with the fuzzy bees, plucking sticky stems from the shrubs and pressing out their intoxicating nectar until the drops escaped and landed on my tongue.

My mother moved away from the kitchen windows and I took the opportunity to make my escape. I grabbed my lunchbox and blindly took off across a field of corn, running as fast as my small legs would take me. The corn was not friendly, scratching my thin skin as fallen ears tripped me while I sprinted.

My tiny heart was pumping fast as I claimed my liberty: I did not need my parents anymore. *Exhilaration!* No more swatting at bugs as I pulled up produce from their garden. *Freedom!* My lungs started to ache and I slowed. *Where is Stephanie's house? I know it's this way.* Fear replaced my confidence.

What if nobody knows I'm missing? What if I'm out here alone? Forever?

I continued walking, certain a tragic fate waited for me. A crop duster flew overhead and I looked up through the stalks; the white sun flared and burned its image into my vision. Hot tears rolled down my flushed face. I brushed the dust and bugs from my hair.

And then I heard voices coming from somewhere nearby.

I started running and the voices became recognizable. I heard Jerry, Stephanie's grandfather. And then I heard my dad.

The rows of corn grabbed my little body and carried me the rest of the way with their green husk arms, finally launching me right into the safety of the middle of Jerry's front yard. I dropped my lunch box and ran to my dad weeping and heaving and apologizing. For as much as I wanted to be on my own, even in the short time I was gone, I came to a clear understanding that I needed someone to know me, to know where I was, and to protect me. That day, the duality of independence and needing others took root in my soft kindergarten heart.

We all need a place to belong. That's something we've been told from preschool to adulthood. Go sit with the kid who sits alone at the lunch table. *We all need a place to belong.* If you're the kid sitting alone at the lunch table, go sit with a group. *We all need a place to belong.* Go meet your new neighbors and invite them over for dinner. *We all need a place to belong.* If you're new to town, why don't you join our church and find a small group and begin serving and sign your kids up for the soccer team?

It may be an overused adage, but it's true. We all need a place to belong. In both the Old and New Testaments, we are given examples of relationships, from the way the Trinity created us in *their* image to stories of close friendships, tribes, marriages, and families. You can't go very far in the Bible without encountering a story about a relationship.

But who can I really trust?

I know I have good friends . . . great friends! There's just no way I could tell them about that secret thing I've hidden far away from the light.

Our church is so big I don't feel like anyone really knows me there. We're in a small group, but it just feels forced.

Sometimes I feel like my closest friends aren't my Christian friends. How is that even possible? I thought since we shared the same faith, we would be there for each other.

Have these thoughts ever crossed your mind or passed through your lips? I know they have mine. Especially in the church, we live in a generation where the word *community* is almost used as much as—if not more than—the Lord's Prayer.

As our developed societies have become more independent,

we've felt the effects of disconnectedness on such a deep level, we're afraid to admit it at times. Even though we have screens and pixels to connect us to anyone, anywhere, anytime, we've never felt more lonely or unhappy in any decade in modern history. We're surrounded by people everywhere we go—both physically and virtually—yet the need to feel that we belong somewhere is undeniably palpable.

Churches and groups within our communities try to find the solution to this ache. From the first time you enter the doors of most churches, you'll hear something about joining a group, getting plugged in, or "doing life together." With the increase in the number of big churches growing larger, this step of intentionality is necessary in order to facilitate relationships. Shaking hands during a Sunday morning service does not provide an environment conducive to cultivating relationships.

We create programs and small groups and activities to introduce people to each other. Often, this structure works well. We meet people with similar interests or in comparable life stages and we form relationships. Our calendar boxes are filled with cookouts and mission trips and Bible studies and girls' nights out. I have heard so many stories of how someone moved to a new town, attended a new church, joined a small group and even though the relationships were new, that small group evolved and proved to be a saving force during a difficult time.

I think that everyone feels the need to belong. Do you? Are you caught fighting the contradiction of needing others, being needed, and wanting to be on your own? Does fear keep you from reaching out to others? Do you want to know how to strengthen the community where you live and love?

"By this all people will know that you are my disciples, if you have love for one another" (John 13:35 ESV). This verse is just one of many scriptures to help push us forward in our quest of desiring genuine relationships and community.

We will not find perfect community on this planet. The only perfect union that exists is between God the Father, Jesus Christ the Son, and the Holy Spirit. Until we continue on into our eternal lives after we pass from this earth, we will never encounter the unadulterated and pure communion in the way it was meant to be experienced before the fall in Eden.

However, we're not called to be perfect or to have perfect relationships. We're urged to seek the kingdom and live holy lives fully dependent on God and in relationship with others. It is first in this dependence on God, and then in our interdependence with other believers as the Spirit unites us, where we can experience a truly joyful and abundant community here on earth as it is in heaven.

2

WHERE ARE YOU?

When the cool evening breezes were blowing, the man and
his wife heard the LORD God walking about in the garden.
So they hid from the LORD God among the trees. Then
the LORD God called to the man, "Where are you?"

—GENESIS 3:8-9 NLT

The first question God ever asked was a simple one. "Where are you?" After Adam and Eve ate from the forbidden tree and realized they had severed their perfect relationship with God, they hid. This cosmic moment was the first time fear and shame entered into our world. It was the catalyst for the duality of dependence and independence. God desired perfect communion with his creation but did not compel them to it. In his mercy, he gave them a choice. As soon as the decision was made to act against his desire, his heart grieved the loss of the unblemished relationship he wove with Adam and Eve. So, he pursued them to restore it.

While walking in the garden in the cool of the day,[1] God asked the question, "Where are you?" to the hiding couple. He could have lashed out at them for their misstep, but his slow and calm demeanor reveals to us thousands of years later how deeply God longs for whole relationships where nothing is missing and nothing is broken. He offered Adam and Eve the opportunity to confess and be reconciled with him, and each other, setting up the prime example for how we should do the same.

Our Relationship with God

We need to know where we are in our relationships. What is your response as God walks with you and asks you, "Where are you?" Are you hiding from him, ashamed? Your mistakes don't have to force you to cover the most vulnerable areas in your life. God sees you, he loves you, and he wants to be in a relationship with you. Through the excruciating and sorrowful sacrifice of his Son, Jesus Christ, on a cross over two thousand years ago, your connection with him doesn't have to be severed. If you don't have this relationship and you want it, the Bible says if we believe in him and confess our need for a relationship with him, he is faithful and just to forgive us and save us from separation from him, creating a bond of salvation that can never be broken.[2] If you choose this now or have made this decision to follow Christ in the past, it doesn't matter how many times you concede to your old faults and habits; God is always waiting for you to answer his question, "Where are you?" with, "I'm right here. Broken. Please, forgive me, Father."

Our Relationship with Others

My best friend in elementary school was Hilary Smith. We bonded over sharing pencils during a test in the first grade and were inseparable until I moved away a few years later. We played piano, liked the color pink, crimped our hair, and preferred books to Barbies. We never fought—ever. But then I moved and life wasn't so simple. Middle school friendships were trickier. Not everyone could be trusted, especially girls. One day, someone would be your best friend and the next day, they'd be your worst enemy. High school was even more complex now that boys were cute and hormones surged. This time period of morphing from a studious teen into an official adult was relationally formative. My associations with others were no longer so casual. Careers, churches, neighborhoods, community-service opportunities, and sports leagues vastly expanded my spectrum of relationships in the last two decades, not to mention the Internet moving from a hardwired desktop to the phone in my pocket. We're connected to so many people at so many levels almost all of the time. If we do find a moment apart from this connectivity, the quietness often causes introspection: *What makes someone a friend? How vulnerable should we be with our small groups? The mom we meet in the line to pick up the kids at school? On our blogs? What do our interactions with others demonstrate?*

Four Categories of Relationships

If you look at how relationships within community function, there are four general categories:

1. Not Vulnerable and Not Committed
2. Vulnerable and Not Committed
3. Committed and Not Vulnerable
4. Committed and Vulnerable

Not Vulnerable and Not Committed	Committed and Not Vulnerable
Vulnerable and Not Committed	Committed and Vulnerable

"VULNERABILITY"

"COMMITMENT"

Not Vulnerable and Not Committed

The people who fall in the not vulnerable and not committed category don't really have any group of people on whom they can depend. They aren't vulnerable, so they keep the details of their lives private, and they're not committed, so they aren't accountable to any person for any reason. If all of your relationships fall in this category, you do not have healthy community.

Vulnerable and Not Committed

Those who are vulnerable and not committed are people who have no problem opening up about their life and their struggles. This is an admirable trait to have, but it is one that needs to be used with discretion. The people in this group, although they can share freely, are not committed to anyone. Though they may be aware of how they can grow, they don't let anyone in to help them.

Committed and Not Vulnerable

When someone is committed but not vulnerable, they have made a step to be in a group or have some consistent relationships in their lives. However, they won't share anything below the surface. Based on my experience with small groups, I usually landed in the "Committed and Not Vulnerable" category.

Committed and Vulnerable

Out of the four groups, those who are committed *and* vulnerable are generally in the healthiest relationships. They are open about the realities of life with a consistent group of people.

Because of the trust built by being committed, the ability to be vulnerable is easier. People in this category can celebrate the good things in life, mourn the losses, and help carry each other as they grow closer to God and to each other. These are the vital relationships every person needs in place. Not every relationship can or should be committed and vulnerable, but we need at least one or two people in order to have healthy, thriving community.

Nothing Stays the Same

While these categories are helpful, it's likely that we don't fit neatly into any one particular category, but instead have tiny pieces of ourselves scattered across all of them; and where we are fluctuates and falls into many midranges rather than one extreme. We are liquid humans living liquid lives, like water sloshing between glasses, souls and minds in constant motion, twirling and shifting, changing—never quite what we were and never quite what we're going to be.

For example: maybe you experienced a genuine connection with others. You were committed and vulnerable, and another person was too. Through good and bad, you carried one another. And then you carried one another again. And again. But then, your husband got an out-of-state job and you moved away, leaving behind the faces you called home, and now you've got no one to carry you and no one to carry. Does that mean you're unhealthy? No. You may be lonely, but that doesn't mean you're sick. It means that the relationships you hunger for haven't yet arrived. But you know you have to be patient. The richest relationships bloom only through time, commitment, and a wide-open mind about who those relationships might be with. Community will come. It may not arrive tomorrow. Or the day after that. It may not show up in the form you expect or be the people you are expecting, but it will come.

The fluidity of relationships works the other way too. Maybe you were committed and vulnerable but something happened, a sudden blindsiding jolt or a slow decomposition, and you were left rejected and hurt. My friend Nicole recently experienced this in a small group. It was a Thursday night and everyone was there, dressed in laughter and smiles, shaking hands and hugging. It felt alive and safe, normal, as it always did. But when a woman lashed out at Nicole's husband, Andrew, yelling at him in front of everyone, calling him a terrible leader, telling him he should step down—that sense of normalcy and safety was broken. After she finished, no one spoke. What was there to say? The meeting ended, and in a flurry of clumsy excuses, everyone slipped through the door, leaving Nicole and Andrew to sort through their confusion over the evening's events alone.

I met with Nicole a few days later, and over lunch she told me the story. Between words, her fork trembled in her hand and her eyes couldn't support the weight of her tears. They began to fall. She was hurt, Andrew too, and they weren't sure what to do. Their safe place was no longer safe. The community they'd been running to was now the very community they wanted to run from. They dreaded the thought of being there again the following week, and they wondered if they needed to step away for a while in order to avoid creating more tension or amplifying their own hurt.

Nicole and Andrew had two options: let the conflict drive them away or drive through the conflict. So they went to their pastor and shared the situation. The pastor thought both couples, along with the pastor and his wife, should meet to see if they could sort through the issue.

The day before the meeting, I called Nicole to see how she was doing. Inside she was still trembling, just as afraid and confused as she was the moment of the initial outburst. But as much as she and Andrew wanted to hide, to cut ties with their community, they wanted even more to reconcile the relationship. They didn't want to let their fears or pain bully them out of doing what they believed to be right. They decided that they weren't going to flee the uncomfortable shadow of conflict. Instead, they were going to stand in that unlit place. They were going to grow. They were going to remain committed and vulnerable even when it would've been easier—much easier—to walk away.

So what happened with Nicole and Andrew's group? Well, everyone met with the pastor and his wife. Tucked together inside his office, they aired their frustrations and hurts, their confusion and ideas. Everyone was heard. Everyone listened to the pastor's thoughts. But the woman who lashed out at Andrew wouldn't back down, so she and her husband opted to leave the small group, and even disappear from the church. While they may have been committed and vulnerable for a while, something (and Nicole never found out what) changed and they chose to remove themselves from the community that they had previously called home.

These types of conflicts happen regularly in relationships. I've found in my own life that the older I get, the more stubborn I am in my beliefs and opinions. Without keeping my ego in check, it would be easy for me to bail on relationships when I didn't agree with someone. The antidote to this problem is humility, plain and simple. The more we claim an unassuming nature, the more we believe the best about people and situations, and the more we try and see others through the lens of love. We are then given the opportunity for our relationships to grow.

It's also important to note that these four categories help us determine where we are in *each* relationship we have. We should always strive to live vulnerably and committed to a group of people, but that doesn't mean we need to share everything or overcommit ourselves in relationships.

I recently met a young man in his early twenties at one of the coffee shops I frequently write from. He boldly sat across the table from me one day and asked what I was doing. I gave him a quick answer and asked his name. Jason. He then asked if I was married. *Oh, no. Please. Do not go here with me right now. Not this.* I gave him my answer and turned back to my computer. I didn't want to be unfriendly, but I knew I wasn't the right person to guide him through romantic relationships. Paying little attention to my over-the-ear headphones, he waved his hand at me and told me how he was going through a devastating breakup with his wife. He laid out all the details. I listened patiently, not really knowing what to say. Patrick, the barista who was on duty, took notice of the awkward situation unfolding. Casually, he interrupted the conversation and I excused myself to go home and make dinner.

The next day, Jason came back and sat in the chair *right next* to where I was working. I briefly said hello and put on my headphones and got to work. *Take the hint, buddy. Please.* The day after that, Jason arrived before I did and was sitting *in the chair* where I usually sit. The café's owner, Ben, watched my reaction through the window when I saw Jason before even opening the café door. He laughed, knowing how protective I am, both of my chair and of my boundaries with people of the opposite sex.

A pastor who also works from the café has known Jason for a long, long time. He's been attempting to care for him and help him take the next right steps, but Jason refuses to act accordingly. Jason lived in the vulnerable and not committed category, and I learned he routinely approached women with his story, going from person to person, thinking their attention and sympathy would heal his broken heart.

As believers, it's always our job to love people; *it's also important to know how to best love them.* As a female, and a stranger, it wouldn't be suitable for me to discuss Jason's marital problems with him. Nor would it be fitting for me to share my struggles with him in hopes that he can help me grow in the stunted areas of my own life. Yes, I can be friendly, I can have a conversation with him, and I can pray for him, but the most loving thing I can do is to point him back to the pastor who is already ministering to him and encourage him to seek community with his church.

We aren't called to live open and committed in every single relationship we encounter. As we walk faithfully with God, we'll be able to discern what kind of relationships we should have with the people who intersect our lives. Some will be naturally deeper; others will never move past an acquaintance. Some we will learn from, and others we will teach. This scattered and uncertain diversity is good. As long as we are listening to how God is moving our spirits and we are obedient to his voice, we can navigate where we are in our relationships with peace and confidence.

3

RELATING IN THE EVERYDAY AND THE CRISIS

When written in Chinese, the word crisis is composed of two characters. One represents danger and the other represents opportunity.

—JOHN F. KENNEDY

What Brings People Together?

Recently my friend Josh shared with me a frustration he faced with his friends. "I can ask eight or ten people who I consider good friends to get together and see a movie or get dinner, and a handful will reply; some don't even respond. But I know if I were to tell them my wife was in a car crash, they'd be at the hospital as quick as they could make it. At least I hope they would. Why is that?"

The honeymoon period for any relationship has a shelf life, and with our shorter attention spans coupled with more demands on our lives, the mundane experience of relationships takes a backseat to whatever is in front of us in the moment. Please don't misunderstand me: I am a large fan of being present where my feet are and stewarding my time and resources well, but everything is in limited supply. However, many things in our lives have slowly masqueraded into our schedules, and we place a high priority on them when maybe we shouldn't.

I've found myself guilty of this priority misplacement before. There was a season in my life when I wouldn't schedule anything social on Thursday nights. Why? Because *The Office* and *30 Rock* were on, and I didn't have a way of recording them to watch them later. There was something about my tradition of a frozen pizza, a cheap glass of wine, and those two television shows that (in my opinion) nothing could replace.

Certainly there's value in having a routine and time to unwind in the way that best refuels us. For me, sometimes a few hours alone is a sacred necessity, but there were many last-minute dinners and spontaneous get-togethers with friends that I declined because of my commitment to a Totino's Pizza and Michael Scott. I'd feel guilty about my decision, so I usually wouldn't even reply to invitations until the next day, as if I didn't see them in time to participate.

Especially as an introvert, I need a friend to keep an eye out for me and make sure I'm not using my personality as an excuse to avoid social situations. I'm not shy or antisocial. I simply like my "me" time . . . maybe a little too much.

Sometimes life is packed fat to the brim. Our schedules, our personalities, our families, or our circumstances don't always allow us the margin to simply "be there" for everyone. My friends Traci and Matt have three kids under the age of five and work a variety of jobs so they can support themselves and be a part of a local ministry. My friend Carly, on the other hand, is a twenty-year-old college student who also works as a nanny. Because of what stage of life they're in, it's usually easier to meet up with Carly on short notice. But that doesn't give me an excuse to not spend time with Traci. We just have to be more intentional on when and where is best for us to meet. We have to plan. We have to try. We have to believe that being together—looking each other in the face, opening the box of our emotions, hearing each other's voice—matters, or we'll never create that space for each other. (Since Traci is incredibly driven by relationships and is focused on intentionally living in vulnerable and committed community, she makes it very easy to connect.)

If Josh's wife were in a car accident, he was fairly certain his friends would be by his side as soon as possible. So what is it that causes us to willingly engage something more traumatic and consuming (like a car accident) than something casual that doesn't require a lot of emotional investment, like seeing a movie? The answer to that lies in how committed and how vulnerable we are willing to be in our relationships. Since the 1950s, sociologists have determined three factors that contribute to forming and keeping genuine friendships: proximity; repeated, unplanned interactions; and settings that encourage people to let their guard down and confide in each other.

With urban sprawl and our culture's need for space and stuff, we've lost many of those factors. Yards fenced in, we live behind walls, separated from the lives next door and miles away from the places we work. The distance causes reduced interactions— those repeated and those unplanned—and it makes us into creatures living in the boxes drawn on our calendars, penciling in appointments and opportunities, trying so hard to squeeze one more thing in.

On a grander scale, people flock to celebrations like weddings and graduations and we can't wait to hold someone's new baby. When something terrible happens, like a car accident, a death, or a personal crisis, compassion and sympathy motivate us to act.

In our modern society, we're generally fixated on adrenaline. It takes something of massive impact in order for us to move if we don't have a healthy perspective on how to engage with those around us in the mundane. When the big thing hits—we see the crisis or the celebration—we want to help or be a part of it because we're wired to do so. If we're the one going through the crisis or having the celebration, it acts as a mirror, showing us how we've been relating in the everyday. Do people come through for us? Do *we let them*? For most of us, if anything falls outside of the "big" things, how we respond in relationships depends on where we are on the grid of being vulnerable and being committed.

Relationships are messy and confusing, and these are generalizations, of course. Oftentimes, the things that make us most willing to jump into the middle of someone's crisis are the small things: the movies, the cookouts, the play dates, the casual back-and-forth greetings in the bread aisle at the grocery store. Those things give us permission to be there in the large things and indicate our devotion and trustworthiness. But nothing is formulaic, especially in relationships.

Using the four categories in the grid from the second chapter, I would have considered myself living my twenties and thirties in between the stages of "Committed and Not Vulnerable" and "Not Committed and Vulnerable," which puts me in two (seemingly) opposite places at once. Why both?

Not Vulnerable and Not Committed	Committed and Not Vulnerable (Anne)
Vulnerable and Not Committed (Anne)	Committed and Vulnerable

"VULNERABILITY"

"COMMITMENT"

I definitely had a group of friends I was consistently committed to, but I was only open with them about my *present* struggles to a very limited degree. I chose not to let them in on the things I was really wrestling with. At the same time, because I was writing and speaking publicly and often, I would be extremely open about my *past* struggles and wounds with people all the time—people I would likely never see again. There was no accountability or consistency in those relationships.

One foot in each camp, I lived a dangerous relational life. I mastered having the appearance of being vulnerable because of what I would share from my past. I also knew the people I could call on to get dinner and catch up and go to concerts with. Since I had a busy social calendar, it looked as though I was participating in rich, genuine community. As I walked this fine line, I avoided the challenges true intimacy brought, and instead I enjoyed only the fun times with my friends. I believed it was a win-win, the best of both worlds, that is, until my own crisis emerged.

My Crisis and Catalyst into Genuine Relationships

"Where do I belong?"

When I turned thirty, my quest to feel like I deeply and intimately belonged somewhere preoccupied me. In the midst of an early midlife crisis, I feared my relational roulette was catching up to me.

I turned inward and searched everywhere between my mind and my heart for the answer. What does "having a place to belong" mean? Is it geographic? Is it based on relationships? I had great relationships all over the country, so could anywhere be that place? I didn't feel a strong affinity to one location over another, so if this place was geographic, had I not found it yet? Was it in my marriage?

My marriage. Since I was twenty-one, I had one constant person by my side: my husband. Maybe home was with him. Maybe that's where I belonged. Whether we lived in Tennessee or Texas, there was always somebody there to hold my hand or to help load a moving truck for a new adventure. After a decade of being together, my marriage was a tree, and I thought the roots were planted deep. Unmovable. Nourished.

Roots bring life or death—usually life. And until we are shocked with death, rarely do we consider the possibility of it. On a winter night at a writing retreat, I had dinner with a family who had farmed the same southern land for over a hundred years. They kindly opened their home to me to ponder and pen a book and released their property for me to wander and wonder on. The farmer left the dinner table abruptly one evening as we finished our steaks and roasted cauliflower. His wife didn't seem at all surprised when he returned carrying in a single root from a pine tree that rivaled him in size and weight. Clumps of stale dirt followed him in, leaving a trail behind the tree all through the kitchen to the dining room. Thin arms of wood escaped from each side of the stump almost wrapping him into an embrace.

The farmer shifted the tree so it leaned on him and he could use his arms. "See this? This stump here? This is where the machine tried to grab this tree to pull it up." Everyone at the table looked at the serrated bark and wood where a tree was once connected.

"Now if you look down"—our gazes followed his finger— "you'll see this one root here." One root the circumference of the tree itself grew out of the bottom. "Pine roots are supposed to go straight down so they can pull up all the water and things they need from deep within the soil any time of the year. That's part of the reason why they stay alive so long.

"But what happens," he continued, "is when one of the roots runs into something in the ground that won't move—a rock or a hard bit of soil that's bad—then the root doesn't grow big or deep, and instead of going down into the earth, it'll jut off to the side here like these skinny ones did." He pointed to slender appendages extruding from the major root.

"So, these are bad roots, and this tree only lived four, maybe five years because it didn't get what it needed. When we saw it dying, we had to pull it up. We didn't know why it was dead until we saw the roots weren't good down below."

My marriage, the tree I once revered as so strong and unaffected, crashed to the ground. Until the day it happened, I thought we were one of the strong ones, one of the trees that would grow tall and old and have branches that would tell stories in quiet forests. But the roots weren't as deep as I had perceived them to be. They hit rocks and bad soil that I was unaware lay hidden below the surface until I saw the tree die. Severed and without warning, the roots let go and the impact of it falling destroyed everything.

This was my crisis. For the first time in many years the left side of my bed was cold. The chest of drawers contained only my laundry and the cup in the bathroom held only one toothbrush. I had two keys to one house, two keys to one car. Writing the words "Not at this address" on his mail and placing it back into a mailbox to be picked up and forwarded was like writing in a foreign language. The socks scattered on the floor were mine; no longer could I complain about his. If my marriage was a tree that crashed to the ground, the grief that followed was a flash flood that swept away it and everything I once cherished as dear and familiar.

Before this crisis, if you asked me if I had a good community to lean on, I would have answered with a confident *yes*. I found my illusion of security in an address book full of friends, thousands of followers on social media, and family members who have always offered me anything I needed at any time. But when the crisis of a divorce entered my life, having an army of friends wasn't enough. I was committed to the right people, but I wasn't vulnerable. I was vulnerable to the wrong people, and I wasn't committed.

I needed to have intimacy with my community. I needed to know I could go before them emotionally naked and ashamed and not be wounded further. I needed to know I could bleed on them, cry on them, and that they could be a life support for me for a season, breathing air into my lungs until I could start breathing on my own again.

Did I have *this* kind of relationship with my community? I wasn't sure. And I was terribly afraid to find out. Even though I needed a vulnerable, consistent community more than any other time in my life, I feared the risks it carried even more than I feared being alone.

It was fight-or-flight time, and I had a choice to make. Would I engage and move into the daunting territory of familiarity and closeness with my friends? Or would I run and isolate in an attempt to protect my heart?

4

CHOOSING THE SHELTER
OF RELATIONSHIPS

Sometimes the only way to return is to go.

—JOSH GARRELS

*L*eaving behind four years of friendships in Nashville, I moved to California, confidently running, fearless in my decision to escape. It was like my runaway attempt when I was in kindergarten, except now I was taller than the corn stalks and could see my way to a new home. The safety I craved appeared to exist in anonymity. I had nothing to prove to anyone, no questions to answer or expectations to meet. Surely this was the right choice. The voice of my independence distorted the voices of my friends in Nashville telling me to stay.

A new job, new friends, and the healing air of the Pacific Ocean blowing through the windows assured me my decision to move to California was a good move to make. After work each day, I drove to the house where I rented a room, perched up on the side of a mountain, and watched the sun drop into the ocean as though it had a five-hundred-pound weight attached to the bottom of it. This was my daily commute, and in spite of the small fortune I spent in tolls each way, it was breathtaking every time.

My days were kept busy at a growing architecture firm where I helped plan events and managed publicity. It was easy to spend twelve hours a day at work finding something to improve or a new project to begin. The busyness didn't bother me at all; in fact, it was a welcome distraction to the grief I was experiencing over the loss of my marriage.

Soon, I found myself hopping from plane to plane, running across airport terminals all over the United States for company events. That accomplished two things: it caused a diversion to the growing pain I was desperately avoiding and it separated me from the beginnings of community I was starting to form in California. In the midst of my new job, I was also on a book tour promoting my second book, *Permission to Speak Freely*, which took me away from my new home in California even more. The stress of being a full-time author and speaker as well as a full-time publicity manager affected me physically, and I lost weight and couldn't sleep most nights. But somehow this was okay.

Only a month and a half into my new life as a California girl, in between a taping for a Christian television broadcast in Texas for my book and an architecture meeting in Arkansas, I sent a text message to my friend Liz. Liz was a friend who I knew would speak words of truth that I was willing to listen to.

CAN I BE HONEST? I'M NOT SURE IF MOVING TO CALIFORNIA
WAS THE RIGHT THING.

A few moments later, she replied.

CAN I CALL YOU?

SURE. GIVE ME FIFTEEN MINUTES TO GET TO MY HOTEL ROOM.

Fifteen minutes later, I sat cross-legged on one of the double beds in my hotel room in Little Rock and waited for Liz to call.

"Why isn't it working out?" she asked.

"I just feel so disconnected. From everything. I'm traveling so much I can't do things with my new friends in California. The time zone makes it hard to connect with my old friends back in Nashville. I'm starting to recognize flight attendants on the Dallas to Orange County segment I'm on every week. I feel as if they know what's going on in my life more than my roommates even do."

"I think moving to California was a mistake," she said without pause.

"Um, well, that's a bold statement."

"What do you want me to tell you, Anne? You're running."

"I just needed a fresh start."

"No, you need to heal."

"I am healing."

"Are you?"

I sat silently, staring at the dated pink floral pattern of the bedspread.

"Go," she said. "Go to the place where it hurts your heart so much you simply can't stand it and you feel like you want to die. Go to the place where the infection is thick and rotting and it smells and burns. You have to go to the bottom of the wound and start there. It is the only way to begin healing. Where is that place for you?"

"Geographically?"

"Yes."

"It's Nashville. It's haunted to me. The ghosts of what should have been are everywhere."

"Now, where's the place where people love you? Where you know you can call someone or just go out to eat with someone? Where's your church home? Is that in California?"

"No, it's in Nashville."

"That's where you need to be."

I resisted. "I can't go back and make it through the pain on my own, and I'm on my own now. I can't do this alone."

"Exactly."

"So what are you saying?"

"I think you need to move back."

"But people will think I failed at this California thing. That I'm a flake."

"That's not true, and it doesn't matter what people think anyway. You need to take time off from writing and speaking and this persona of "Anne Jackson" you've become, and you need to heal. And you need people who you let into that wound. You need to bare it all. Ask a handful of people to commit to go into that infection with you and help you work your way out. It sounds forced, but ask them for eighteen months of prayer and counsel and accountability. Give them the freedom to say no, but when they say yes, you've got to give them the permission to enter into your life in the most vulnerable way. You asked me what I think you should do. And that's what I think you should do."

"Okay," I quietly responded.

"Are you going to do this?"

"Yes."

"When?"

"I'll start asking people tomorrow."

"You just let me in. God's created us to live like this, Anne. You can do this."

I knew she was right on every account. I knew I was running from my grief. I knew I needed to go back to Nashville and heal the wounds there before I could truly move on—geographically or otherwise. I knew I needed to let others carry me for a while. After all, that's what I'd been proselytizing in *Permission to Speak Freely*. "We get to carry each other,"[1] I penned, quoting the song "One" by U2. Was I willing to? If I chose to stay on the path I was on, I would survive. I would have a great job and money and friends to spend time with and eventually the pain would be pushed so far down I wouldn't feel it anymore. I could be committed and not vulnerable.

However, if I chose to let people into the sludge of my very soul; if I asked them to willingly climb down to my rock bottom and help me find my way back up, the amount of work and pain I would face would be intolerable—maybe even emotionally fatal—if I ended up abandoned. *Again*.

There would be risk.

How much life could I really live if I allowed my grief to win and destroy the abundance and joy that God has promised me? Do I give up or do I give myself up and trust others and trust God with this process?

That night was a restless one as the two options battled in my mind. I knew the right answer, but fear would crash over it whenever I was close to choosing it. I couldn't sleep. I felt sick to my stomach and sat on the bathroom floor in the hotel. I was hot and cold at the same time. I curled up next to the toilet, afraid I might vomit. A fight was definitely being fought and I was caught in the middle. As the morning sun quietly brightened my room, I pulled out my laptop and sent an e-mail to fifteen very different people asking them to meet me at the bottom of my busted, muddled, seemingly impossible wound. They would be required to sacrifice time and energy for me. I would submit myself to them for guidance. I would be accountable to them in every area of my life, from my finances to my faith to my relationships and my career. I gave them access to it all.

Ten wrote back almost immediately and said yes.

We Need Structure for Survival

Many people think genuine community only exists when it's birthed from something organic. "You can't force community. Structure kills it." In some instances, that may be true. However, what Liz recommended by setting this structure in place was an opportunity for intentional intimacy to begin within my community.

Being a bit free-spirited, I sometimes wonder how anything organic or healthy can be cultivated in an overorganized environment. Being *so* intentional seems to be the equivalent of genetically modifying how relationships should function. As my own crisis progressed from shock to grief, I realized I'd been sending myself a false message when I was telling myself a support system should just develop naturally (because if not, then those people probably didn't truly care anyway). That was a concept I could choose to continue believing, or I could go against my wiring and make a different choice. I could be intentional.

Yes, it took a little push, but changing the story I was telling myself—that "real relationships" only happen out of thin air—was one of the most significant decisions of my adult life, not only because it placed me on a trajectory to discover and be a part of committed and vulnerable relationships, but it also showed me it is never too late to change the messages you tell yourself are true.

Once, when I was chatting with a mentor of mine, I mentioned I was having a difficult time being patient. The attitude of entitlement that developed from that season was a result of my hereditary German stubbornness. But my mentor challenged me and asked me to consider another option. *What if I wasn't stubborn?* Maybe that's just what I believed about myself so I considered it to be true.

Though I may be German, I don't have to be stubborn. I grew up hearing how stubborn I was, and eventually it became a part of how I acted and reacted in life. *Well, I'm just stubborn. Deal with it.*

Knowing the perception of my stubbornness is something I can change helps me realize I can *make a choice* not to be stubborn.

The same applies to our approach in relationships. Maybe you've heard the message "Nobody can be trusted" or "You have to earn my respect." Maybe life has even shown you more pain than relief when it comes to your relationships with family, friends, or coworkers. Perhaps you were bullied and you believe nobody likes you, or you feel intimidated by others. Have the words "I can do this on my own" taken root into your soul?

If you want to be deliberate about pursuing relationships that scratch beyond the surface but fight fears of insecurity, control, and the inability to trust, please take heart. It's never too late to change the story you're telling yourself. *You can make a choice.*

My decision to form an intentional community (going against my own temperament) was based on mutual choices: mine to be vulnerable and committed to this group and theirs to receive me with unconditional grace and offer their guidance and love. A line in the sand had to be drawn. I needed to make the choice and step forward in faith. If I never made the first choice to reach out and ask people to help, I doubt any true healing would have started. We cannot leave something as necessary as relationships with others up to chance. *We must be intentional.*

Life Is Breaking Through

When I asked my group of friends—this team—to commit to helping me through the crisis of my marriage ending, I never doubted that it was a wise step to finding health and wholeness in my relationship with God and others. However, I didn't realize at the time how life-saving and life-giving this decision would be.

In fact, it wasn't until two years after this group formed that I was able to look back and see the big picture of how God worked through this community. Life didn't become easier. In fact, there were actually more moments of heartache and shadows than I expected. However, that pain was a gift.

Through these relationships—and others that followed—I discovered a joy that was far beyond the happiness I ever hoped for, and I wanted everyone to have hope that the same joy existed for them too. As I shared my story with friends, I realized there were specific patterns and themes that appeared throughout this time of planned community.

There were decisions I made that were steps into vulnerability and commitment, and there were responses from my friends that helped me take those steps along the way. The mosaic of our choices and the context in which they were made and the dynamics of where each unique person was in his or her own life allowed these relationships to grow from a structured place to a truly flourishing and genuine community that had no constraint.

It began to grow so unpredictably in such a beautiful and

holy way that it reminded me of when I ran away from home as a child, and I hid under the blooms of that honeysuckle plant that overtook our cement porch with its life and wonder. My community was now my shelter and it was under this canopy where I began to find a refuge and sweetness. I knew I did not need to run or hide anymore.

Part 2

....

Needing and Being Somebody to Lean On

When we give cheerfully and accept
gratefully, everyone is blessed.

—MAYA ANGELOU

As time passed after my divorce, I saw two distinct roles within my community. When I was in my most desperate time, I was in a place where I *needed* community. I needed to lean on others. And I saw the times when my friends were in the role of *being* that community. They were available for me to lean on them.

Fellowship is composed of people who need people and of people who need to help people. When I looked closer, I could see themes in both roles that played a sacred game of give and take.

Of needing help and of helping. Of surrendering and of accepting. Our lives fluctuate between *needing community* and *being community*. How can we live our best regardless of where on the map we find our feet? How can we belong and include others so they know they are not journeying alone? Can we find joy as we move in between needing and being?

5

FALLING INTO SURRENDER

The friend who can be silent with us in a moment of
despair and confusion, who can stay with us in an hour
of grief and bereavement, who can tolerate not knowing,
not curing, not healing and face with us the reality of
our powerlessness, this is the friend who cares.

—HENRI NOUWEN, *OUT OF SOLITUDE*

If my mother could have given birth to me in the church, she would have. I imagine her reading a Bible story to a classroom of kids in between Lamaze breathing and pushing.

"And then Noah . . ."

breathe, breathe, breathe . . . breathe, breathe, breathe

" . . . started to put the animals on the ark . . ."

breathe, breathe, breathe . . . breathe, breathe, breathe

" . . . two by . . . TWO!"

She breathes and pushes, and I enter into the world surrounded by 1980s children's Bible storybooks and felt boards.

And while that's only a slight exaggeration (I was born at Harris Methodist Hospital in Fort Worth, Texas), I spent almost every day of my childhood at church; whether it was a worship service, a Sunday school class, youth group, or helping my dad print and fold the weekly bulletin.

When I was sixteen, my dad left the ministry. A combination of West Texas obstinacy and old-time church politics were foreshadowing a church split, so he resigned tearfully from the pulpit in order to do everything in his power to preserve peace. As he quietly read his formal resignation letter, gnarled-spirited deacons whose grandfathers laid the first bricks cheered hearty *Amens!* from the pews. We withdrew from the church and my dad retreated into a depression, rarely leaving our home.

For the first time in my life, I experienced life outside of the church. We moved from West Texas back to the Dallas area, and my family stopped attending services regularly. Much to my surprise, I didn't miss it. Sleeping in on Sundays was divine. Having Wednesday nights to do homework instead of going to youth group relieved the stress I was carrying around as an overachieving honors student.

Maybe I don't need church. I can just do this faith thing on my own.

I didn't once feel guilty for keeping my relationship with God a private affair. When I was angry at my circumstances, it was easy to ignore him. When I messed up, I would return and beg his forgiveness.

I was nineteen years old when my grandfather was in his

final hours of life after a long fight with cancer. He called each of his grandchildren into his room one at a time. I leaned over his fragile frame in order to hear the last words he would ever speak to me. He didn't have the strength to open his eyes and could barely whisper the five words he spoke.

"Never give up on church."[1]

I told him I wouldn't. But in order to keep my promise, I'd need to start making some significant changes in my life.

A few years had passed since the last time I went to church, and I wasn't comfortable returning to my former status as a second-row Baptist. Instead, I intellectualized my promise to my grandfather and started defining the word *church* loosely. Any time I'd hang out with another person who was a believer, I considered it church. I thought, theologically speaking, in its most basic form, this was a magic formula that created church. Two believers gathered? Check. Holy Spirit? Check. Instant church.[2] Right?

God, of course, was with us—it's not like he fled at my theological misinterpretation to prove a point. But this wasn't the church my grandfather wanted me to love and pursue and commit myself to. It was my fear of intimacy coupled with my desire for independence. I wanted to live a not-committed and not-vulnerable lifestyle, because, well, I was selfish.

Over time and with conviction, I slowly let my walls down and tried to make good on my pledge to my grandfather. My actions stemmed more from wanting to keep my promise than actually being obedient to what God wanted, but eventually my change of behavior caused a change in my heart and I fell in love with the church in all of her magnificence and her flaws. I surrendered, slowly and timidly, to the call of unity God has placed on all his children.

Surrender doesn't come easily, especially when we've been hurt in the past. When we think about giving in to something we used to push away from us, we're met with an internal resistance. It's easy to justify our actions that keep us walking the line between self-sufficiency and surrender.

As I've spent time talking to other Christians, and some who have even—in their own words—"left the faith," I've noticed a pattern so common it's become perfectly acceptable without question. Someone enters into a relationship with a community of faith, and the programs or the legalism or the perceived lack of authenticity turns them away. Many people do exactly what I did when I wanted to have "church" and *only* consider unstructured, organic community to be true and real.

I completely understand this feeling. As a preacher's kid, it's my modus operandi to call into question anything a church does. I've called into question formality and structure my entire life. When it's time to point out the church's flaws, I've been happy to be the first to step up to the microphone and describe the brokenness . . . *for the sake of redemption, of course.* At least that's what I said and what I thought I believed.

Over the last couple of years, I took a step back from speaking up and instead chose to listen. I heard a lot of things similar to what I was saying about the messiness of the church. People were debating the role the church had in their everyday lives, many of them choosing to land either squarely in the vulnerable-and-not-committed category or the committed-and-not-vulnerable category. Those who were vulnerable and not committed felt as if community could exist without intentionality or structure. Those who fell into the committed and not-vulnerable grouping were generally plugged into a church home but thought the structure that existed prevented them from finding genuine, healthy, vulnerable relationships. The one commonality in these differing opinions was whichever side they were on, they believed it was the correct side.

When you remove yourself from the ground level and look at what's happening on a broader scale, it becomes quite easy to see that this disunity is not what God calls us to in Scripture. Period. No matter where you fall in the scales of theology, we—the Church—are called to unity. None of us will ever agree on everything, but this isn't about what we believe. It's about how we love. And it's about how we surrender to the greater work of unity.

A Fight to Surrender

I have a friend who's an atheist but who stays in tune to what's happening in different faiths. As he looked at the Western Christian culture, it was easy for him to see the things that divide us. He bluntly asked me, "How can everyone in your faith be so divided yet claim to follow the same God?"

Good question.

I truly believe this break in our unity is a strategic plan of the enemy. If people who don't know the specifics of what this pastor preaches or what that denomination believes but they see how such small things cause such large divisions, Satan is accomplishing exactly what he set out to do. Many Christians today have fallen into a culture that tells us we have the right to believe whatever we want to believe and are entitled to be right in our beliefs. And because of the surplus of platforms from which we can speak, never before our generation has a group of people been able to voice their beliefs so loud and clear.

Some see this as progress. I see it as subtle (and at times, not so subtle) expressions of selfishness. Where in our proclamations and defenses of our personal beliefs do we find humility? Where do we find surrender?

We don't.

In order to have healthy relationships with God and others, *we must surrender*. To God, we surrender our desire to live our lives for ourselves. Only by dying to ourselves—our human nature— can we truly live in the identity of who God created us to be. In order to embrace the person we are meant to be, we must let go of the person, the ego, we created.

With others, we surrender our need to be right. We surrender our need to be heard. We trust in the paradox of finding peace in serving instead of demanding to be served and complaining about it when we aren't.

Someone once said, "It's difficult to offend a humble man," and I've used this to measure my own sense of entitlement. How easily am I offended? That's usually an equal measure to how prideful I am in the moment.

Pride. Selfishness. Fear. Pain. Lack of trust. Needing to be in control. It's difficult to surrender for many reasons. But in order to have genuine, Christlike relationships with others, we all need to mutually surrender. The tricky part of this, and sometimes what makes relationships muddled, is the fact that you can't force another person to be humble or to surrender. When only one person is living surrendered, the relationship isn't healthy and interdependent. The person who is living a surrendered life is, by nature, more vulnerable and more open to be wounded than the person who is not surrendered. This doesn't sound fair, but this is a sacrifice we must accept if we are to choose to live vulnerably and humbly with others. Yes, we must have healthy boundaries with others, but we must not build up walls. We must choose surrender and vulnerability over our fears of being hurt.

When we look at the bottom line of surrender, it boils down to a decision to love others *and* to allow yourself to be loved. Surrender requires risk. Dr. Brené Brown, who has been researching vulnerability in relationships for decades, has found some profound realizations that show us that rewarding relationships are often prevented because of our inability to surrender. "In order for connection to happen, we have to allow ourselves to be seen," she says. "The people who have a strong a sense of love and belonging believe they're worthy of love and belonging."

What prevents us from surrendering? "The thing that keeps us out of connection is our fear that we're not worthy of connection. Have the courage to be imperfect," she challenges.[3]

Surrender goes against our very nature to be independent. Surrender indicates we willingly choose to rely on others. We must rewire our thinking to recognize that needing another person (and being the person someone else needs) is not a weakness; it only strengthens us.

....

Once I had put my team in place, I thought the extra intentionality would somehow make the relationships function with ease. Inviting these friends into such a vulnerable part of my life and asking them to go beyond convenience and commit to helping me for a year and a half was the most difficult part, right?

Not really. Making the original ask was certainly one of the most difficult things I did, but little did I know it was only going to get harder before it got easier.

A couple of weeks after the team formed, we all decided it was best for me to move back from California to Nashville as Liz recommended earlier. I was afraid of disappointing the company, my new friends, and my roommates, but I had surrendered to my team and to their guidance that I desperately needed. One rare day when my boss and I happened to be in the office at the same time, I pulled him aside into a conference room.

"I'm going to need to submit my letter of resignation. I need to move back to Nashville. I can wait until my ninety-day probationary period is over if that makes it easier for Human Resources, but I need to go back and heal."

"I completely understand. When you have a chance, go talk

to Lisa in HR and let her know. I'm sorry it didn't work out and we'll miss having you."

"Thanks for taking a chance on me. Maybe I needed to experience this before I recognized how much healing I truly need to do."

I felt a sense of failure on muttering the word *resignation*. I knew I had to fight the lie that I was giving up, because I was instead choosing a more difficult road.

I was open with my team at the architecture firm about the state I was in and we made an exit strategy. The company I worked for had Christian values and most of the people who worked there were Christians. They knew about my sudden divorce and my grief and my quick move to California and showed me nothing but grace once they knew I would be leaving. I still had about six weeks left on the job, so I started making slow plans to return to Nashville, shopping for apartments and used furniture on Craigslist.

About a month before I was scheduled to move, I went to a conference in Florida to manage the firm's publicity at an event. I traveled alone, which was the norm, and on a Tuesday morning joined up with several of our vendors to set up for the occasion. As I scurried around, checking things off my to-do list, I stopped in a moment of dizziness. The pen in my hand trembled along with my fingers as my hand shook. I'd been so busy all day that I had forgotten to eat, so I grabbed some food out of a catering room and sat down. Eating it quickly didn't relieve my shakiness much, and my stomach cramped at the mistreatment. Noticing my pale face and painful countenance, one of my colleagues realized I wasn't feeling well and offered to take over the rest of the day's chores for me. He insisted, I resisted, but I slowly and stubbornly retreated to the hotel room and took a nap.

After I woke up several hours later, I didn't feel any better. My heart was racing and I was in a cold sweat. I couldn't breathe and my fingers started going numb. I was still light-headed and dizzy and my stomach felt as though it was full of thorns and grease. What physical symptoms I had manifested emotionally.

The last time I experienced a panic attack was in my mid-twenties, but I recognized its symptoms right away. Remembering what my counselor said to do if one ever hit again, I sat down, began some deep breathing, and quietly repeated the words, "He keeps in perfect peace whose mind is stayed on him."[4] An hour later, the panic was only increasing.

It was dark outside, and I felt sick. I spent most of the night in the bathroom, squeezed into a ball, my arms twitching as I wrapped them under my knees. Here I was in *another* hotel room far away from home curled up on *another* bathroom floor, shaking and teetering and on the edge of vomiting. *At least I was consistent at something*, I thought.

I realized as I stared at the sloppy caulking job at the bottom of the bathtub that it didn't matter where I went: I could not continue without people intervening in my life.

Early the next morning, I e-mailed my team.

I write you today to seek wisdom and/or prayers, whichever you have to offer.

As time continues to pass, the more and more I find

myself in unexpected grief. It's not unusual for me to be getting tea or coffee somewhere and start to cry. The last few nights I've woken up around 3 a.m. and have cried until the sun comes up. I spent most of last night on the bathroom floor crying, half expecting to throw up.

I am hurting very, very badly.

I am not sure if this is just another stage of grief or stress. I've been unable to function at work (my boss has been as understanding as possible), but with all seriousness, I really don't know how I can go on in the current state that I'm in.

I am flying home early today from Florida as the emotional and physical symptoms are too much for me to carry for the next three days alone here. I'm wondering if I am hurting myself by waiting to move back to Nashville until June or if that needs to be a more immediate step. My finances always play the role of devil's advocate. Have I committed myself to something that isn't healthy for me to do? How am I supposed to pay rent and my bills when I'm barely able to drag myself out of bed and shower and face the world?

I am at a loss. I honestly have no idea what the best "next step" is except for me to fly back to California today. I don't know what comes after that.

Please feel free to call me today or e-mail a response. I'm so sorry for any extra burden this causes you.

Love and thanks,
Anne Marie

Five minutes later, my phone rang. My friend Gail was on the other side. I often refer to Gail as "My Nashville Mom," as she and her husband, Michael, have five grown daughters and she's treated me like one of her own ever since we met.

"Are you okay?" she asked, clearly referring to the e-mail I sent.

"I'm a bit better than last night, but I'm still flying back to California as soon as I can."

"When's the soonest you can move back to Nashville?"

"Well, I don't have a place to live yet. Or a job."

"You can live with us until you figure it out. How soon can you get here?" she repeated.

"I guess I could leave my job on Monday and start driving Tuesday. It'll take me a few days to drive, so, by next weekend?"

My answer was more of a question.

"That's good with us. I love you and we are praying for you and call me any time. Any time."

"Gail, I don't know what to say."

"You don't need to say anything. Just hurry and get back home."

Home. The word alone brought the slightest bit of hope.

....

The next three days were a blur. Lisa from Human Resources and I became friends over the short amount of time I worked at the architecture firm. As soon as I returned to California, I went directly to her office and told her what I needed to do.

"I think that's a very wise idea. Take the next couple days off from work as sick days, enjoy the rest of the time you have with the ocean and your friends, sit on a bench on Balboa Island and watch people and eat ice cream. I'm technically one of your superiors, so you have to do what I say," she ordered me with a smile. "We'll have a meeting Monday morning so you can officially resign and you'll be free to go."

Following Lisa's instructions, I went to Balboa Island. I watched people. It was April, and California was just as beautiful as it was when I moved in February. I was going to miss that. Against my better judgment and without regard to my lactose intolerance, I ate too much ice cream. Monday morning, I met with Lisa and my boss and left the company with their blessing and prayers. That night, my roommates helped me load my car up with the few things I owned. Tuesday morning, I drove through Arizona. Wednesday, I made it to Midland, Texas. Thursday, I stopped in Dallas to see my family. By Friday, I was back in Nashville.

Gail and Michael helped me carry the few boxes and suitcases I had to one of their guest rooms. We had a glass of wine and spoke of nothing of any great significance, yet that very act was more than significant. We just sat with each other, none of us knowing exactly what was next, other than to get a good night's rest.

I walked up the stairs and slid into a bed that was not my own in a house that was not my own with a family who, biologically, was not my own. But our souls were beginning to be knit together in a special, unidentifiable way. I closed my eyes and breathed a prayer of gratitude before finally surrendering to my first deep sleep in almost a year.

The next morning, I woke with the sun sneaking in the cracks between the shades and the window frame and with a spirit of vulnerability and surrender I finally *chose* to embrace.

6

THE IMPORTANCE OF DIVERSITY

*I know now that a friend isn't someone who lets us be
ourselves. No! A friend is someone who will die to keep
us from becoming anyone else, someone who fights for us
against a world that is constantly trying to shrink us into
shelved canisters labeled "how you're supposed to be." A
friend does everything possible to make sure we become
who we are made to be—nothing less, nothing more.*

—JOSH JAMES RIEBOCK, *HEROES AND MONSTERS*

The moon watched through a window in the den at Michael
and Gail's house. I spent the evening making sure my bills
were paid and trying to be the wise person I always attempt to be
by making a plan for the next couple of months. My calculator
told me things weren't adding up, and I unsuccessfully argued
with it. I wasn't quite ready for the emotional effort it would take
to re-enter my writing and speaking career, so I took a temporary

job at a cancer care clinic where I listened to stories of hope and fear and pain and miracles as I punched in diagnosis codes and insurance numbers into an old Dell computer. The job at the cancer care clinic provided just enough money to pay my monthly bills. My savings account drained into decimals. I found myself feeling like I was in an out-of-control tsunami, grasping for anything that would help me survive.

I gathered up my mess from the den and headed to my room to go to bed. I wanted to sleep forever, dreading the sunrise that would remind me of the uncertainties that were reentering my life. Michael and Gail came home from a late dinner, and Gail's maternal instinct was on high alert. She walked through the back door and straight up the stairs to where I was in my flurry of utility bills and check stubs.

"How are you doing?" she asked.

Here was a perfect example of a small choice I was required to make in order to pursue a life of being truly vulnerable and fully known. Do I let her in? Or do I pretend everything's fine? My decision was the tough one: I was honest with her. What followed wasn't my most graceful moment.

In one long breath, I exhaled my worries. "Gail, I. Am. Struggling. My expenses are just increasing and my income is nowhere near what it used to be. I am wrecked over the fact I am not spending as much time writing as I think I need to—simply due to the number of hours in a day. With my work schedule being so random, I can't commit the hours to writing like I was able to in my past life. I feel like my identity has been stripped away. I wasn't meant to take insurance cards. I thought God told me to write. I'm thirty-one years old and I don't even own a fork. Literally. I feel like I have nothing."

Gail listened patiently. She thought for a moment and said something that broke through my fear-induced tsunami and weighed me down with truth, grounding me back in reality.

"Do you want relief? Or do you want to be healed?"

Of course, in that moment, I wanted relief. There was a pain I recognized in the absence of my trusting God with everything—from money to my purpose and meaning in life.

But what I wanted deep down was wholeness. Completeness. Gail spoke words of wisdom over me from Scripture about the now and the future and the truth of what God wills, what he desires for me and how he holds everything together.

It was a profound moment, washing me with peace even now as I recall it. But what made this interaction so divine was *who* God was using to speak to me in that moment of need.

When I was on the phone with my friend Liz in the hotel room in Little Rock and she suggested I put together this team, she didn't mention anything about who should be on it—just that they should be people I trust who were spiritually mature and walking in a growing faith relationship. As I scanned through my contacts, I wasn't considering each person's background, what church they went to, how old they were, or even what they'd been through in their own lives. I simply chose those who stood out to me as trustworthy and wise. Those two characteristics made for a solid foundation from which to build.

As I interacted with the people who were on my team, I realized there were certain people who, because of their uniqueness, filled certain roles. This diversity only made this fellowship stronger.

Gail is a mother of five grown girls. She and her husband Michael have been married for more than thirty-five years. It was no wonder her mothering instincts kicked in and she was able to speak into my life directly and from a place of wisdom. As a mom, I'm sure her radar to be on the lookout to nourish, heal, and encourage (not to mention her incredible hospitality) was fine-tuned.

Michael, Gail's husband, is an executive, and a creative one at that. Not only did Michael help with the "dad type" questions I'd have (like where to get my blown-out tire fixed), but because we both write and speak, I was able to go to him for advice on what to do with my career. Because writing and speaking is so personal to me, for the first year and a half after my divorce, I wasn't in a place where I could pour into others. Michael's personality is similar to mine, so he was able to help me gauge when I was emotionally ready to dive back in. Even now, when I have questions about what next steps I need to take in my work or when it comes to buying or renting a house, Michael's advice is invaluable.

Not everyone on my team is older and married, though. Lindsey and Annie are both close to my age—Annie's a little younger; Lindsey's a little older—and both are great girls who can have fun getting a glass of wine or talking about theology. They helped me navigate the new and strangely complex world of being a single girl in her thirties. We were able to relate in similar life stages with many of the same interests. My relationships with

Annie and Lindsey are fun and life-giving as well as challenging and honest.

My friend Matt is a forty-something remarried businessman—a father by day and a theatrical romantic by night. Matt gave me wisdom when the dream of finding a life partner came into the picture. Being an extrovert, he also got me out of the house and on several occasions invited me to share dinner with his family. My former wedding anniversary is a particularly tough day for me, and Matt knew it—he *experienced* it when he went through the first few years following his divorce. When it approached, instead of just asking how I was doing or saying he was praying for me that day, he invited me to go on an all-day kayaking adventure in Michigan with his whole family. Matt is also incredibly straightforward and honest. When he saw me making an impulsive decision that would have had long-term consequences, he immediately called me and reminded me of my commitment to myself and to the team. He was right. I had to realign my plans because of his bold and just confrontation (done with love and grace). And because of that, he probably saved me from a lot of unnecessary pain.

When it comes to shedding tears, most of that happened at my dear friend Shelia's house. That may sound like a depressing statement; it's anything but—it's holy and sacred and safe. Shelia, a wife, a mother, and a grandmother in her forties is a kindred spirit. She's a poet, a teacher, a musician, a runner, a true artist, and a dear friend. What makes her soul have so much power is the depth of both joy and pain she's endured in her life. We have always danced a dance of vulnerability, revealing wounds and healed-over scars, usually over muffins and tea at a quaint bakery in downtown Franklin. When dark memories rose up like monsters, I knew Shelia would understand and fearlessly fight them with me. Many times, she whisked me away to the sitting area of her bedroom and her daughter brought us steaming apple cider and Kleenex. Few words were spoken, but the ones that were linger in my memory and fill me with hope even now. Shelia taught me to respect the purpose pain has and to not grieve things not yet lost.

Gail, Michael, Annie, Lindsey, Matt, and Shelia all live in Nashville, so it was rather easy to be intentional about spending time with each other. But not everyone on my team lived in Tennessee. Location is important when you have intentional relationships; however, depending on the people, having a few friends on geographic fringes adds a different perspective because they don't see your life day in and day out. It just so happened the other people on my team lived on opposite sides of the country.

Bob, a married lawyer in his fifties; Susan, a married author and actress in her forties; and Tony, a pastor and husband in his thirties, all live in Southern California. Bob, Susan, and Tony were around when the initial shock of my marriage ending hit and responded in distinctive ways. Bob, his wife, and his community poured healing words into my heart that was bleeding out. Susan gave me a bed for a while and told me where to find good pizza and asked me difficult questions that needed to be asked.

Tony pastored me with wisdom. Our contact wasn't frequent, but when that spirit-to-spirit connection happened, it happened profoundly. I would be stuck in the middle of some dilemma, and Tony would contact me from out of the blue with no knowledge of my struggle and give me a word that could only be from God.

Ben, an artist and entrepreneur, and his wife live near Virginia Beach. Before my crisis hit, Ben was already challenging me. In 2008 when my persona as a blogger was at its peak, in between two praise songs at a conference, he leaned over and asked me what would happen if I ever quit blogging. I said I couldn't—that it was the only thing I knew. I didn't realize it then, but he was showing me I was finding my identity in the wrong place. His words have stayed with me since that day, and I'll never forget the day I took my popular blog offline and rested from social media in general for a couple years. Ben has always been able to see where I am, but also where I could be . . . *if.* He plants those "if" questions in my mind—that has always been a gift that encourages me to dream when I feel stuck.

Admittedly, the last few pages served two purposes: first, to honor my team for being my team. They deserve so much more than my thanks and a few pages in a book, and hopefully as our relationships continue through the years, we'll continue nurturing them. And second, to show you that diversity in a community is good and necessary. If all my friends were girls in their thirties, I wouldn't get the wisdom that comes from the life lived of my friends who are a bit older. If everyone were single, I wouldn't learn lessons from those who are married. Matt was divorced and could understand the unique grief that comes with having that as a part of your story. Most people went to different churches—Orthodox, Catholic, Lutheran, nondenominational,

Anglican—and that brought different spiritual influences that were beautiful. Seeing those who are parents interact with their children helped me see how God interacts with me as his child. There are a handful of other friends, including Liz, who I leaned on regularly during this time and who weren't an official part of my team, but their presence to me was healing and brought even deeper levels of understanding and personality.

When looking at the men Jesus surrounded himself with—his closest community, the disciples—I see the diversity in those he chose. Peter was impulsive, but out of all the other disciples, was the only one who had faith to take a step onto the sea to walk on water. Matthew was a tax collector who liked making enemies. Simon—the zealot—was passionate and often appeared to have a bit of an angry personality. Thomas was likely on the other end of the spectrum. He doubted and required proof of Jesus's scars so he could believe it was truly his Lord who had risen from the dead.

However, the disciples' personalities described to us in Scripture don't stay consistent during Jesus's ministry. Impulsive Peter is later called "the Rock." Thomas's doubt turned into belief. As they walked with this grace-filled, divine man, their lives were transformed. They began taking on characteristics of the Rabbi they followed.

Like the disciples, our dispositions can change because of the words and actions that surround us. I let in all of the things my team brought to the whirlwind that was carrying me, and instead of being wrapped in fear and worry, I found that hospitality and wisdom and encouragement and challenge and truth and bravery and love replaced all the debris that was damaging my hope. Who these people are changed me, manipulated my very DNA into something bright and giving of life.

My desire to always have a cozy bed and a warm meal ready for someone is a direct result of Gail's hospitality. Making wise business and financial decisions comes from Michael. Lindsey's inclusive spirit has inspired me to hold my arms open wide. Annie's tenacity and faith remind me that I can grit my teeth and push forward in any situation while keeping a true smile on my face. Matt gives me a lens to view how families and relationships can be restored. Shelia's ability to see beauty everywhere keeps my eyes open and looking. Bob's generosity and whimsy reminds me to have fun and to always say yes to the scary things. Susan keeps my feet planted in reality and helps me find the sacred things in the mundane. Tony reminds me that God can use someone thousands of miles away to speak into my life and that I should pay attention to his nudges when I need to speak up. And Ben inspires me to have expectation in an unknown and exciting future.

These things are the daily bread that fed me when I was hungry and they gave me hope when I was lacking. Dr. Archibald Hart says someone's depletion is the accumulation of his or her strain over the course of time. If that is true, I must believe the opposite is accurate as well. Maybe one person's restoration is the accumulation of many inimitable others' fullness over time.

7

LOSING CONTROL AND
EMBRACING COMMITMENT

*Lonely and helpless, we cannot be at peace with others because
we are not at peace with ourselves, and we cannot be at peace
with ourselves because we are not at peace with God.*

—THOMAS MERTON

When you surrender something, you give it away or give it up. When you commit something, you give part of yourself away with it. You relinquish your full control over it and entrust its expectations to someone else.

I asked my friend Mark, whose love for etymology fascinates me to no end, about the root meaning of the word *commitment*. He replied, "Commitment, at its root, is the idea of sending a pledge of faith into the future."

Even as I write this manuscript, my heart struggles with commitment. Circumstances in our lives push us to clasp our hands tightly around the people or places or things we love, those things we'd be devastated if we lost. As I look back through events in my life, there are certainly significant moments where things were completely out of control and something life-altering transpired.

My grandmother passing away when I was six.

The tornado that hit our house when I was twelve.

Those awful deacons who split the church my family loved when I was sixteen.

The youth pastor who sexually abused me my junior year of high school.

My friend Matthew suddenly dying when I was nineteen.

My dad's emergency heart surgery when I was twenty-six.

Learning I had to have heart surgery when I was twenty-nine.

My divorce at thirty.

Learning of a family member's suicide attempt when I was thirty-one.

My second heart surgery at thirty-two.

Free fall. Fear. Reaching and grasping for anything. Out of control. Even if I couldn't control the specific event, I wanted to control *something*. The way I ate food (or didn't). My friends. My family. Money. My career.

I was afraid to surrender to the true meaning of commitment: the entrusting of my life to someone else. Even God.

Commitment to God

There have been times in my life when, in desperation, I would shout in my spirit to God, asking him to take away my fear of losing control. I knew I couldn't have control over anything, and the foundations on which I built that idol shattered into dust. It was frightening and I'd hold on even tighter, sometimes to the point where the things I held so tightly died.

An indignant anger replaced the peace. *God, I asked you to take away my fear of losing control, but instead you just took away the things I held dear!*

A calm voice responded and reminded me of the difference between surrender and commitment. I had, at one time or another, *surrendered* my fear of losing control to him, but I had never *committed* it to him.

When I started to write this book, I took a rare moment of unhurriedness to escape to a place in South Georgia where my mobile phone fought to find a signal and there was no Netflix to tempt me away from writing. I hunkered down in my friends' cabin and got to work, writing.

There wasn't a soul in sight. My friends, Mr. Burt and Mrs. Careen, the cabin owners, were away in Florida on their own retreat, so when my fingers would cramp from typing, I'd go out and wander on their miles and miles of land. On my first day there, I hopped in their Jeep and followed tire tracks through grassy fields that led me to the far side of their property. There sat a lake and a small boathouse, both vacant for the winter.

After a few days of writing blissfully, the winds changed. My morning had been rough. I woke up to the sound of a heavy thunderstorm, disappointed I wouldn't be able to go on a hike I planned. In my crumpled pajamas and bare feet, I shuffled across the small house from the bedroom to the couch and waited for my e-mail to load over their slow Internet connection. In it was a message with the subject line containing the words an author dreads: *Out of Print.*

Because of the economy (and a million other things to which I'm not privy, I'm sure), the publisher of my first book decided it wasn't a good business decision to reprint it anymore. No longer would it ship to bookstores or be available online. In fact, they didn't even have any copies left in the warehouse. The news sent unenthusiastic voices through my head reeling with lies. *You're not good enough to be a "real" writer. Nobody cares about what you do. Why do you even try?*

As I played those harsh words over and over and over again, I conceded to my urge to escape. I ran out into the rain and started up the Jeep. I pressed down hard on the gas pedal, flinging gravel behind me as I peeled out of the driveway and headed to the lake. It seemed like the only reasonable place to go.

Tears fell on my jeans as I bounced in the Jeep heading faster (and faster) to the lake. Back home, I drive a compact Toyota on paved roads in quaint neighborhoods. On the farm, I learned I could relinquish frustration by accelerating over small piles of rock and earth. With the windshield wipers going as fast as they could, I could barely see the marks in the grass that showed me what path to take. Slowly, the tire tracks disappeared and I found myself in the middle of a field with no sense of direction. Which way was the lake? The farmhouse? *Could I not do anything right?*

Discouraged further, I drove around for half an hour trying to find some semblance of a trail to follow. The gas tank mocked me with the lever plummeting below the red "E" with each dip in the landscape. As I squinted through the downpour, I saw a gate that led to one of the country roads bordering the farm.

The gate was locked. I got out of the Jeep and considered my options. I could turn around and try to find my way back and risk running out of gas in a place where nobody would find me and with no cell phone signal to call for help, or I could attempt to drive around the gate over some small bushes and across a narrow ditch.

"I'm in a Jeep for heaven's sake," I muttered through the rain. I got back in and started to navigate my way over the small ravine around one of the poles. Branches from the shrubs crunched under the tires, making noises that sent icy shocks up my spine. Fearing I was causing some kind of irreparable damage to the Jeep, I accelerated, hoping to move around the gate and hurry home.

But when I pressed the gas pedal, nothing happened. Well, nothing except the tires spinning and slinging red mud as high as the soft top on the Jeep. I tried putting it in reverse. Nothing. Drive? Nothing. I got out and inspected the scenario. The rain fell so hard that day the ground didn't know what to do with it. My invincible Jeep was now stuck in the mud—and I still had no idea what direction to take back to the farm.

I found some sticks that I wrestled off of bushes and put them under the tires, praying for traction. Forward. Reverse. No movement. Just more mud. After ten minutes of trying (and getting soaked in the process), an old blue pickup truck traveling down the country road pulled over and two older gentlemen in overalls with trucker hats got out and walked over to me in the rain.

"Seems like you have a problem there, missy."

I can only imagine what I looked like. Nice jeans, a T-shirt, and grey Tom's shoes now wrecked by mud. I noticed a few scratches on my feet from the branches, blood beginning to drip down.

I agreed. One of the men casually walked over to the gate and pulled the pole out of the wet ground, rendering the gate ineffective at its protective duties.

Just. Like. That.

Really? I thought. *All I had to do was pull the pole out?* Hiding my embarrassment, I politely mumbled a "Thank you."

"You don't think you're gonna get that Jeep out of the mud now do you?"

Right. There was still this issue of the mud.

"I'll tell you what," one of them said. "You trade me that Jeep for my truck and I'll get you unstuck."

I made some kind of joke about city girls and country gentlemen and prayed he truly didn't want to take my friends' Jeep. Then I let him have a try at setting it free from its muddy disposition.

"Oh, look Billy!" one man exclaimed as he slid in the driver's seat. "She has four-wheel drive!"

How did I not see that? The other farmer pushed around a stick shift and within moments, he had the Jeep unstuck and out on the road, threatening to keep it, rolling forward a few feet at a time teasing me. Billy opened the door to the passenger side and pretended to get in. That would top off an already terrible day, watching two sweaty farmers steal my friends' Jeep.

I thanked both of them and hurried them out of the Jeep.

Miraculously, I found my way back to the farm where I dragged my defeated, soggy body back into the cabin.

That's it. I'm done. I give up.

Under the watchful eye of a mounted deer's head, I slumped onto the couch, not even caring enough to change out of my wet clothes. I pulled out a few mismatched blankets and wrapped myself in them to fight off the chill. For two hours, my heart was in a battle of wills. There was my will, my desire to engage in even more controlling behavior. I could fight this *Out of Print* thing. Start a social media war with the publisher. Hire lawyers. My heart hurt and I wanted to protect it, to prove to myself (and the publishing world) that somehow I was worthy to write books.

Then there was God's will, his desire for me to disengage in my fight for control and to surrender and commit it to him. His longing was for me to find my identity in him alone by resting in him and trusting him regardless of my circumstances.

I refused. It wasn't a completely conscious decision. I never once thought, "God, no. I am *not* giving you my career and my calling and trusting you with it." I just chose to not let it move from my hands to his hands, even though mine were sore from holding on so tight for so long.

Somehow during this mêlée, my phone picked up a bar of signal and a single text message emerged. It was from Mrs. Careen. Because of all the storms, they were returning home early and wanted to know if I'd like to join them for a late-night meal after they arrived. Even though my eyes and body and soul were weary from crying, I said yes.

Mr. Burt managed to grill some steak and chicken in the

damp air, and Mrs. Careen provided all the extra fixings and wine and we sat down to share our latest capers, including my embarrassing Jeep story. We reclined with full stomachs and Mrs. Careen started clearing away the dishes. Mr. Burt moved around the table, from my left, to sit straight across from me. He looked me square in the face and without hesitation in his deep southern accent boldly said, "Anne Marie, fear and control have a bondage over your life. And as the head of this house and the steward of this land, I feel as if it's my responsibility to make sure that what you came in with, you don't leave with."

Interesting, isn't it? While I was writing on fear and surrender and commitment and losing control, proclaiming in this very book how we need to be vulnerable with others and live authentically, I was refusing to heed my own message. I knew in my head and in my heart that I should confess my failing, but I chose to keep silent.

What a glorious example of how the Spirit uses relationships to bring healing and wholeness. There was no reason on earth that Mr. Burt could have known what I was thinking and fighting, but because we were united in and through Christ, the Spirit convicted him to confront me about it and challenge me to not just surrender, but to also commit these things to God's care as well.

Mr. Burt asked me to go back to the cabin and write a list of all of the things I was afraid of—the people who hurt me (or could), the situations that scared me, and even the things that didn't exist yet. What was I afraid would happen if I gave up control? I was to write them down and then, after breakfast the next morning, he and Mrs. Careen and I would drive out to the lake and commit them to God.

....

Creating the list wasn't hard. My fears were so familiar to me I knew them like companions. Exhausted, I went to bed, slightly nervous about what the next morning would bring.

The sun was shining and Mrs. Careen drove me as we followed Mr. Burt out to the lake. I clearly saw the right path and felt even more embarrassed over getting the Jeep stuck. "Oh, everyone gets the Jeep stuck on the farm. It's a rite of passage," Mrs. Careen assured me. We walked to the boathouse and sat down. Mr. Burt asked how I was doing and I admitted my skepticism.

"I've given this over to God before. I can't expect for him to just show up because we're on a pretty lake and take this away from me."

He pulled out a black, well-worn Bible and carefully turned its pages to Hebrews. He read Hebrews 11:1, *"Now faith is confidence in what we hope for and assurance about what we do not see."*

I could see in his Bible various notes and faded highlighter marks. He read it again. He asked me to read it. I did with a shaky voice.

"You see, Anne, you're doing your job. You're right. There isn't anything magical or special about this lake. But we're symbolically releasing this to God today. You're doing your job in this and trusting God to take it. You're committing it to him. And in faith, because you can't see it for yourself yet, you believe him to take it. Because he wants you to have a sound mind. He promises you that."

We took the list and burned it in a shallow, rusty container that was on the table and walked to the side of the house where the dock was. He prayed over me as Mrs. Careen dropped oil on my forehead symbolizing healing and the presence of the Holy Spirit. The wind carried the ashes of my list into the lake where they vanished.

I didn't feel any different, but I knew feelings weren't of much importance in this moment. With the ashes of my list now mixed into soil and water, I could not retrieve them. They were committed to the lake. And now I had a permanent reminder of my own commitment to God. I gave him my fear and desire to control, and though I may still be reminded of them and tempted to take them back, I can't. They belong to him. And in faith and with hope, I believe that.

Committing to Others

When we make a commitment to healthy relationships, we're not only causing change within ourselves, we're turning over control to others. To some, commitment feels like the opposite of surrender. Commitment means *you* are making a choice, therefore keeping some kind of control.

I like to think that commitment is surrendering something and then taking it one step further. It's the giving away of something but with the hope of permanence in mind. Yes, we are in control when we choose to commit something; in making that decision, we surrender control.

Few things are scarier than the feeling of losing control. Again, this is where we can take that fearful leap and rewire our minds with truth. When we commit to pursuing the desires God has for us relationally, we aren't losing control. We're making the choice to give it away in surrender. It's a sacrifice, and I'd argue a holy one at that.

When we feel as though we have control over any area of our lives, what we're experiencing is actually an illusion of control. Sure, we may be able to plan things (and most of the time, planning things is a wise idea!), but how often do the things we plan work out the way we want? Sometimes they do, and in those seasons when the unexpected rarely shakes our lives it may seem like a quiet blessing. Yet if we take these calm moments and think it's by some work of our own that they exist, later on, it only causes us more pain. If we hold on to the notion that we're in control, when crisis hits, we become disoriented.

We are not in control.

Part of my pledge to my team was to take care of myself spiritually (by resting, going to church, serving, and spending time in Scripture and prayer), physically (exercising, eating right, not using food or drink as coping mechanisms, and getting the right amount of sleep), relationally (by frequently getting together with others), emotionally (by going to counseling and reading books that spoke healing into my situation), and financially (by spending my money wisely and asking them for advice when I needed it).

I realize the commitments I made to my team were a little out of the ordinary and quite specific, but I was in a place where I couldn't manage even the smallest things on my own. I needed their guidance, with the understanding that their advising came from a place of being nourished by the Spirit. These commitments weren't only about the actions themselves; they were about giving away my control to this group of people and them pledging to hold me to the things I committed, so that over time and into the future I would have my hands held open, prepared to receive healing when the time arrived.

At the lowest point in my grief, after I returned to Nashville, most days it was hard to get out of bed and go outside. I felt so displaced and lonely. However, since I was living with Michael and Gail and they were on my team, it wasn't easy to stay in that isolation.

Graciously, they would ask me how I was sleeping, or if I could take their dog for a walk, or if I could join them for dinner. I didn't think I had the energy to do anything, but by taking these tiny steps, I found it created a desire in me to do more.

Life-giving relationships require commitment and vulnerability from each person in the relationship. If my team wasn't committed to holding me to the things I promised, it would be easy for me to give up and take control back. At the same time, if I wasn't open and honest with my team about what I was doing, I likely wouldn't see any progress in my healing. Real growth requires absolute permission: permission to ask and to be asked the hard questions.

Commitment isn't an easy thing, especially in a world where we want instant gratification or we perceive a greener pasture and wander over to it. Our relationships are more nomadic and sporadic than ever. We tend to see relationship as something that has to be convenient for us in order for it to work. Instead relationships should actually require us to step beyond convenience into being uncomfortable. If we aren't feeling growing pains as we move into more committed relationships, that's an indicator that those relationships aren't becoming stronger. Commitment causes discomfort, and it also causes growth.

I lived with Michael and Gail for several months, and even in that short time with their support, and by daily surrendering to what I committed, I slowly started standing on my own two feet.

The temptation, of course, was to revert back to my old way of thinking: the reason everything was going okay is because I was doing the right things. I started feeling comfortable again, and in control.

PRACTICING VULNERABILITY

When you love someone . . . truly love them, friend or lover,
you lay your heart open to them. You give them a part of
yourself that you give to no one else, and you let them inside
a part of you that only they can hurt—you literally hand
them the razor with a map of where to cut deepest and
most painfully on your heart and soul. And when they do
strike, it's crippling—like having your heart carved out.

—SHERRILYN KENYON, *DEVIL MAY CRY*

The summer months after I returned to Nashville were filled with good conversations, consistent Tuesday night dinners with a group of friends who lived in my neighborhood, meeting new people, and driving over rolling hills through constellations of fireflies on the back roads of Williamson County. Life had a rhythm—sometimes erratic—but a rhythm nevertheless. I went to work, did my job, and then headed home. I'd try my hand at writing something so I could remember how when it was time for me to do it again. I read books and tried to find some kind of inspiration or muse. I went on my first date in over a decade and quickly realized I wasn't ready to date. I moved into my own tiny two-room apartment off an old house in an up-and-coming (read: cheap and with amenities like a barbed-wire fence) part of West Nashville. I went on hikes. I used all my frequent-flyer miles to visit friends in New York, Los Angeles, and many places in between. Life didn't feel desperate. The pain was slowly subsiding. I thought I had found a new normal.

This new normal, however, lacked color and music and fire. Sure, there wasn't a bitter pain biting through my chest any more, but there wasn't much joy. Or happiness. Or hope. The only emotion I recognized was longing for protection. I wanted to feel arms around me, keeping me safe and helping me not feel lonely in the nighttime hours. Once the day quieted and the distractions faded with the sun, I realized I still went to sleep alone and still woke up alone. I was still grieving what should have been.

I am a creature of habit, and most nights my routine was the same: read, turn off my lamp, pray, feel alone, pray again, wait, resign, and eventually float off to a restless sleep. My twin-size bed was as big as the ocean, and I was lost in the middle of it. Even in Tennessee's summer heat, I turned on my insufficient window unit as cold as it could blast and rolled myself into as many blankets as I could stand so I would feel the weight of something—of anything—surrounding me.

My prayers were not answered in the way I wanted, and I never understood why.

One of the jobs I picked up in addition to working at the cancer care clinic was as a freelance editor for books other authors wrote. A woman telling her story about loneliness wrote one of these books. I initially sympathized with common moments in her narrative—a divorce, her grief—but I began to resent the differences. Someone gave her several years of salary up front so she could begin her writing and speaking ministry; at my lowest, I had ninety-nine cents in my checking account. As I read through the retelling of God's provision for her, I allowed his provision for me to be painted envy-green. At the end of one of her chapters, I read how she felt God physically wrap her up in his arms as she would settle into bed each night. He held her as she went to sleep. I closed my laptop in frustration. *That was my prayer! Why did you give it to her? Why not me?*

To say I floundered in self-pity is an understatement. I wanted respite in every imaginable way and thought God was holding back his mercy from me. In hindsight, that simple correlation was my problem. I equated mercy with relief.

What would have been my eight-year anniversary was approaching, and with each day I felt more alone and desired to be held, to be comforted. I started thinking of people I knew, more accurately *men* I knew, who perhaps could provide some kind of relief to this longing. I did not want sex or even intimacy. I just wanted a hand to hold or a strong arm to embrace me, simply to feel like I was safe in my smallness and that my existence did not repulse anyone. I realized I was reverting back to my life before marriage, a time when I found comfort in unhealthy places and when a man would provide me the temporary feeling of belonging and worth by using words he did not mean and protection that was not real.

Again, I faced a choice. I could keep quiet about these thoughts between the voices in my head and the desires in my heart and not breathe a word of them to anyone and try my best to not act on them, knowing I probably would give in. But no. That would drive me crazy. I could also go out and get what I wanted, knowing it would not fix the pain in me and would likely cause even more regret, and then I'd keep that a secret. Or I could open up to the people who promised they would be there for me without judgment.

The night before my anniversary I sent a text to Annie and Lindsey that said:

HEY GALS, TOMORROW WOULD HAVE BEEN MY ANNIVERSARY AND I AM FEELING SO LONELY AND SO DESIRING TO BE WITH SOMEONE. IF MY THOUGHTS ARE ANY INDICATION OF WHAT I MAY DO, I DO NOT TRUST MYSELF ENOUGH TO AVOID OLD COPING MECHANISMS THAT WILL ONLY CAUSE MORE PAIN. ARE YOU FREE TO HANG OUT WITH ME TOMORROW NIGHT AND KEEP ME OUT OF TROUBLE? I'M SO EMBARRASSED TO EVEN ASK, BUT I NEED YOU.

Within just a few minutes plans were made for dinner, and over pizza I shared the quiet desires that persisted after my every thought. After dinner, I went to another friend's house to be with more people and stay out of harm's way. All of us gathered in the living room to watch a movie, and I snuck away to message

Matt, needing reassurance that I could survive future anniversaries without the need to numb myself or find comfort in a place I should not ever walk.

WILL MY ANNIVERSARY FEEL THIS BAD EVERY YEAR?

IT GETS BETTER IN TIME, I PROMISE.

I prayed I would one day find his words to be true and perhaps even be able to forget those days that brought reminders of what should have been.

As the worst of the summer heat faded and the days slowly became shorter and less humid, I received an e-mail from a pastor at a small church in Illinois. We had only talked once when his family's church hosted a stop on my *Permission to Speak Freely* book tour, and he wanted to see if I was up for returning.

Hi Anne,

Do you remember my wife Tasha and me? You came to Lincoln on your book tour, and I am the pastor here. I decided to follow you on Twitter. Isn't that how these things always go?

I have a proposal for you. Come up for a little while. I haven't developed the idea much, but I think it could be very cool for the congregation and the community. What if you came to Lincoln for a few weeks? You could be a writer/ artist/theologian in residence, teach some classes, do a small group, read something in worship. This idea would take more resources and logistics, but I think offers lots of possibilities for us, if not you. I realize Lincoln is out of the way and sort of un-glamorous, but I also think it could be an interesting place to try some different things.

Peace,

Phil & Tasha

My job at the cancer care clinic was coming to an end in August, and my fall didn't hold much promise for continued work. Was I ready to be up front and ministering to others yet? A large part of my heart missed it: meeting new people, seeing a new place, and getting to serve in a way that's unique to them. But barbs of fear reminded me of how spiritually fragile I felt. Over a year had passed since I'd sensed the nearness of God. Would I be able to act as his vessel at this church?

I decided to go for a hike and ask him directly.

On the southwest side of Nashville is a state park, Radnor Lake. It was my sanctuary in Nashville, the place I knew I had the best chance of hearing God. There was something hallowed in the way my feet traversed almost silently over the mulched trails, and the canopy of trees provided a barrier from the city noise, protecting the creatures that took refuge beneath it.

I walked the first familiar mile, asking God if I was ready, my spirit quieted, listening. Nothing. I walked to the lake, always still and depending on the season, usually covered in moss. Nothing.

You always meet me here. Where are you?

After a few hours passed, I gave up. I reached into my

backpack and pulled out my phone to take a picture of the lake, perhaps to remember the silence. I posted it online and Shelia replied back in a text message.

"Drink it deeply," she said, about the colors in the trees and the well-worn paths of the forest.

"I think I forgot how," I responded. "Will it return to me?"

My concern was valid. I stared, parched and thirsty, into the faded and falling leaves. I lay down on a bench and prayed maybe the earth would take me and embrace me as her own. The only thing I felt was the wood supporting me, nothing else.

"Yes, beloved," was her answer to my worry. "Oh, yes. You are in the right place. Breathe slowly. Let go. Receive."

Receive what? I tried. As dusk softened the sunset, I got up from the bench and continued on the trail, aware of the beauty around me. But I was numb to it, maybe even jealous of the communion between the sky and its reflection in the lake, the songs of the animals, and the family of trees with their interwoven branches.

I didn't understand the lack of answers, or maybe I didn't hear them. I wanted a response. I wanted to feel in control. I wanted direction. Since there were no burning bushes saying no and because I needed work for the fall, after I returned home, I replied,

Phil & Tasha,

Hey there! Yes—of course! Lincoln!

I'll be honest—at first the idea of coming up wasn't appealing (no offense; I'm a city girl), but the more I have thought about your offer since I read it, the more appealing it has become. Let's do it!

Anne

Lincoln, Illinois, was a six-hour drive from Nashville. I arrived and settled in. I helped lead an All Saints service. I read Scripture during services and gave the benediction each Sunday morning. I taught a women's Bible study. I carved pumpkins with Phil and Tasha's kids and went to an apple orchard. I met with a group of pastors and talked about the future of the church, pretending to have some wise words to say. It was all very spiritual and yet maybe because I believed I held God's full attention, I decided it was the perfect time to air my grievances with him.

Over a year had passed since my divorce, and God's silence was still too much for me. In my hotel room one evening, I pulled the blackout curtains tight at seven and went face down on the white duvet and mountain of pillows. Drawing my knees into my stomach in some type of variation of the fetal position, I wept. For hours. *Why? Why? Why? Where are you? I don't understand.*

Still nothing. Still silence. The numbness morphed into anger. I drew myself up onto my knees and faced the headboard of the bed. I clinched my thighs in my hands and dug my fingernails into my white flesh, drawing the smallest bit of blood. I considered a drastic choice—a choice that would go against everything I learned a Christian should do.

Flashbacks of Sunday school and Bible verses and my life as a good preacher's daughter—as a woman in ministry—went flying behind my eyes. In between the flares of my anger and hurt were memories of holy moments. I reflected on the night of my ordination when I was twenty-nine, the elders of my church leaning over me and putting their hands on my head, my shoulders, kneeling beside me as they commissioned me. I thought of my grandfather on his deathbed, telling me to never give up. The moments of grace given to me by friends and the times my heart grew supple and receptive. How many times did I kneel at the altar at St. Bartholomew's? *"Anne, the body of Christ broken for you; the blood of Christ shed for you."* I ate the bread. I drank the wine. My tears were in the crevices of the wooden floor in front of the place I would kneel Sunday after Sunday.

But somehow, this reel of sacred and lovely memories wasn't enough.

So much. So much. So much fury and grief and silence and loudness and it was all in a vacuum that finally opened, a breaking point that was broken, and everything went soaring from the secret places where they hid into a very material atmosphere.

In that moment, I didn't care. I didn't quietly renounce him. I yelled. I put my fist to the wall in the hotel room. Not only did I swear God off, I swore *at* God, dropping four-letter words that were difficult for me to hear as they slipped out of my mouth. I threw the pillows as hard as I could across the room screaming at him to leave me alone.

I am through. With. You.

I stared at the pillows on the floor and felt my right hand throb from its violent contact with the wall. With a red, swollen face, my eyes eventually closed and I fell asleep.

That night, my sleep was tempered with a fear and anxiety I

never experienced before. I woke up at six thirty in the morning regretting every moment of the night before; realizing I did a terrible, terrible thing. One that maybe couldn't be reversed. I told God to leave me.

I turned on my computer and did a search for "Catholic churches." I couldn't tell Phil what happened. I still had a week left of serving at his church. He'd probably cut me loose (and rightfully so). But I needed to confess. I needed some form of penitence. An atonement. I called the church and a voice came on the answering machine with their office hours. I waited until eight o'clock and called again. A sweet older woman's voice greeted me on the other line. I set up confession with a Catholic priest in a town where nobody knew me and begged him to give me some way to earn back grace. I am not even Catholic.

I walked through the side door of the church at noon and met the priest. He was from Tanzania and in seminary. Because I wasn't Catholic, he couldn't offer me confession. But he offered me a seat in his office and wise, wise words.

My battle with God the night before was not a way for God to opt out but a way for me to allow him in even further. I was not the prodigal son. I was the older brother. Like the father in that parable in Luke, God came outside his celebration to see why I wasn't joining in. I pushed my list of demands on him. I didn't want *him*; I wanted relief. The prodigal son was covered in an obvious filth when his father met him: the slop of pigs and sweat and dirt from his humiliating journey home. I was covered in my own loam, though not so material: my fear, my control, my entitlement, my cursing, my rejection of him.

I could not earn his love, yet I could not remove it from me either. We cannot remove God's love from us. It is like, as Rilke says, one of those "things that will not ever leave."

It is cosmic, the way he loves us; how we sit in periods of silence and fly through periods of joy. The emptiness I felt for so long was merely my soul in rotation, much like the earth on its axis. It is the sun and the stars. Pain and joy do not leave us. We will experience seasons where life is full and bright and spectacular and perhaps causes a person or two to stop and see the light that is coming from inside of us by no action of our own wills. There will also be periods where the night sky is wholly black and starless. But over time, one by one, stars will reappear and bring their luster and hope.

God's withholding of an emotional reprieve was the most profound mercy I could have ever asked for. Mercy brings both comfort and pain. Sometimes it is soft and peaceful and swaddles us. Sometimes it surrounds us with silence, leaving us feeling forgotten and rejected. This mercy is the most difficult to accept, but I've learned it's also the most imperative to transformation.

I still feel shame when I look back to the night in the hotel room where I punched the wall and cursed the One who loves me most, always and for infinity. *Doubting Anne.* It was a test of faith like Thomas, where I demanded proof of his presence. I had to trust that he would love me, shattered pieces included. I may have told him to leave, but I was opening my heart to him. I was being vulnerable with the One who already knows each and every hair on my head. It was a revelation of sorts, perhaps a new term of growth.

Before my time in Lincoln, I thought I was okay again. I had believed from the time in spring after I left California and I submitted myself to my team in Nashville, from the time I went to church and prayed in spite of the quietness, all the way to the autumn when I was in that small Illinois town, that I was doing fine. And maybe for a short season, I was. But God did not want to leave me there in the state of being fine. The silence was the mercy of God, showing me it was time to shed one more layer of my old wine skin and feel my pain. Not because God is a sadist, but because if I couldn't be naked and unashamed before him, I would never truly expose myself to others. God never rejoices in our suffering; he grows us through it.

Vulnerability with others is terrifying. We liken being vulnerable with being honest. Honesty is a part of vulnerability, yes, but it is the safer element. Vulnerability has much less comfortable meanings: wounding, to wound, pluck, to tear, capable of being seized, defenseless.[1]

A great misunderstanding in the world is that we must wait until we feel safe to be vulnerable with other people. They must earn our trust and show us they will not take our wounds and cause them to bleed more. We misconstrue the wisdom of guarding our hearts, our life's wellspring, as a command for us to form a fortress around them.

We are never safe from pain, and safety has nothing to do with vulnerability.

Vulnerability will hurt. When you speak it, you will have to force the words to form. Our nature is to hide and to protect ourselves from pain, from grief, from shame. It is a paradox: once we realize being vulnerable is never safe, we are then free to be vulnerable. We guard our hearts by giving them to the Guardian. We accept the fact that hurt will come. We see wounds as gifts. When this dramatic shift in our spirit occurs, fear no longer controls us.

We can surrender; we can commit. A community can form around us and we can let others into the spaces in between the very best and the very worst of who we are. Yet to be this vulnerable is insane and it is exactly what unites us to others. The pain that comes with this vulnerability is only a shadow compared to the joy that follows.

It was my last night in Lincoln and a small group from the church where I was serving took me out to the nicest restaurant in town, the Owl's Roost. It was part library, part coffee shop, and part eatery. The dozen of us dined on roast and apple cobbler. We said our final good-byes. A couple in their seventies handed me a gift bag that contained a four-inch-tall green-and-gold bust of Abraham Lincoln. Someone else gave me a book. One woman gave me a rock. She placed it in my palm and closed my fingers around it. "It's for when you don't know what to do," she said, and walked away.

I waited until she left before I looked, not quite sure what to expect. I turned the rock over in my hand. The word *Hope* was written in Wite-Out.

I walked to my car, placed the gift bag and books in my backseat, and placed the Hope rock in the center console and heard it fall through the collection of random pens, broken sunglasses, forgotten CDs, and gum wrappers. I drove to the hotel and went to sleep, not quite sure what was next when I returned to Nashville but feeling strangely at peace about not knowing.

9

PERSEVERING THROUGH PAIN

From the ground up
I'll keep building
Houses into homes.
'cause if trust is ribbon
Then patience ties it
In a perfect bow.

—SLEEPING AT LAST, "BRIGHT AND EARLY"

*H*ealing is disorganized and chaotic and unpredictable. Even after my time in Lincoln, I would feel happy and invincible and whole and my elated heart would sing through my skin. These are the days where I put on a little extra makeup or wore a new shirt or painted my toenails because everything felt right on the inside and somehow I believed my new pink pedicure was representative of the lightness I felt. This sentiment would last a couple of days, maybe even a couple of weeks, until something small sent me into a tailspin. A friend wouldn't reply to a text message or I would burn a batch of cookies I was baking or I made a dumb mistake like missing my exit on the highway by fifteen miles, and I would go from having indestructible cheer to feeling so, so stupid and so, so hopeless.

Thoughts would pass through my mind telling me how much easier the world would spin if my inability to function as a human was removed from the planet. I didn't want to die, but I wasn't sure if I wanted to live. I went to Dose, the coffee shop down the road from my house, and before I ordered, I would walk back to my car in tears. I craved isolation. I left my phone on silent and turned it upside down so I didn't have to answer my friends' inquiries about my well-being. Living on my own again gave me easy access to isolation, and it was not a freedom I could be trusted with.

In late December, on and off for thirty-six hours, I sat in an old green recliner I acquired from a friend and drank whiskey and Coke that was left at my house from a Christmas party. I ate a bag of sweet potato fries and watched two seasons of *Mad Men*. I was the queen of melodrama, sunken deep into my recliner throne.

This is where I'll die. I have let everyone down. I should let them in. But I can't anymore. I cannot drag them to the bottom with me again. I realized I was being dramatic and selfish, and I refused to acknowledge the strength I had to pull myself up and do the right thing.

It had been seven months since my team formed, and a month since returning from Illinois. How much more healing was there to do? I did everything right. I lost God and I found him, and I made mistakes and I learned from them. I closed down and opened up to others, and yet this cycle continued in spite of the moments of growth and the moments of backtracking. I pulled a pink blanket around me in the recliner. I was not drunk, but I was not alert. Why could I not find some plane of consistency? I closed my eyes.

I am reminded of the apostle Paul's war within; his convoluted thrashing between holiness and self-loathing. It is a battle only those who follow Christ can understand. While those who don't have a relationship with God can and do fight conflicts with their inner desires—winning and losing—Christians fight on a different battleground. We know the truth in us and feel the Spirit gently moving us toward holiness, yet our human desires fight to remain in control.

I imagine Paul, exasperated and ever so close to giving up as he sits down to pen these words: *Why can't I get it right?*

> So the trouble is not with the law, for it is spiritual and good. The trouble is with me, for I am all too human, a slave to sin. I don't really understand myself, for I want to do what is right, but I don't do it. Instead, I do what I hate. But if I know that what I am doing is wrong, this shows that I agree that the law is good. So I am not the one doing wrong; it is sin living in me that does it. (Rom. 7:14–17 NLT)

I feel the heat of his anger toward himself, his fire to do what's obedient, his abhorrence of his failing, and his love of

God; they all collide in a confusing tirade that only makes sense to us because of our own turmoil and desperation.

> And I know that nothing good lives in me, that is, in my sinful nature. I want to do what is right, but I can't. (v. 18 NLT)

I give up.

> I want to do what is good, but I don't. I don't want to do what is wrong, but I do it anyway. But if I do what I don't want to do, I am not really the one doing wrong; it is sin living in me that does it. (vv. 19–20 NLT)

There is a monster living in me.

> I have discovered this principle of life—that when I want to do what is right, I inevitably do what is wrong. I love God's law with all my heart. But there is another power within me that is at war with my mind. This power makes me a slave to the sin that is still within me. Oh, what a miserable person I am! Who will free me from this life that is dominated by sin and death? (vv. 21–24 NLT)

I am trapped by my demise.

This passage is so relatable (and so frequently referenced) because of how it simply shows us that *we are not alone*. We are not alone as we fight and we fail. For centuries even the most notable Christians never grasped perfection. Neither will we.

Paul's final words in this passage are where we need to rest:

"Thank God! The answer is in Jesus Christ our Lord" (v. 25 NLT).

That is where we rest.

That is where we find hope.

That is where and why and how we can persevere.

Can I get up out of this recliner, put away my pity and despair, recognize I embody both saint and sinner, and move forward? Yes. I can. The answer is not in me. It is not even in the actions or the warring of my choices or the voices in my head. The answer is simply in Jesus Christ, our hope.

I understand this appears to be one of those "Sunday school" answers modern believers avoid because of their overuse or their simplicity, but what else do we have left when we have nothing? Yes, people have used the name of Jesus as an escape rather than embraced it and declared it for the infinite power it has. But we cannot let our aversion to using platitudes diminish the power those truths have in our lives.

We can persevere because of Jesus Christ, our hope.

Earlier in spring, right before I moved back to Nashville, I was in California for Holy Week and Susan asked me to spend it with her at her church in Pasadena. I went to St. James on the evening of Palm Sunday—a sparsely attended service lit mainly by the glow of candles. It was one week before Easter.

I took my seat next to Susan in an old, wooden pew and looked up at the light fixture above me. It was identical to the ones at St. Bartholomew's. The familiarity painted a grin on my face as I sang.

We stood up during the rest of the songs and I allowed my hands to grasp the back of the pew in front of me, feeling each and every crack in the smooth wood. I wondered how many people had clinched the pew because of how lonely they were, just waiting to hear something—anything—from God.

"Lord Jesus Christ, Son of God, have mercy on me, a sinner." I imagine a nervous mom who's worried about her son, rubbing her thumbs across the top.

"Lord Jesus Christ, Son of God, have mercy on me, a sinner." I imagine a girl new to L.A., trying to find work and praying she doesn't lose her apartment.

"Lord Jesus Christ, Son of God, have mercy on me, a sinner." I imagine a husband whose wife has just passed away, leaving him and their children behind.

"Lord Jesus Christ, Son of God, have mercy on me, a sinner." I think of the person who just found out the test came back positive for cancer.

"Lord Jesus Christ, Son of God, have mercy on me, a sinner."

No doubt this pew had received its share of sweaty palms and fingers over its days. The wood was smooth and worn because of human flesh, slowly, weekly, perhaps daily, rubbing over it, desperately grasping for anything.

The priest stood up to share on the gospel of Matthew. He spoke about Jesus's last week on earth as a man. Scripture says

Jesus groaned in his spirit. My mind wandered: *What was he thinking in those final days?*

Did each minute for him pass by faster? When the temperature dropped and the night settled in, did his heart beat just a little faster, knowing he was one day closer to the end and yet at the same time, the beginning? The divine humanity we're told about in stories doesn't leave me doubting there was some kind of holy fear within him. Did he close his eyes and anticipate what each crack of a leather whip would feel like as it tore through his skin? Did he wonder how heavy the cross would be and how it would feel to have the sharp edges of old wood bury into his flesh? Did he dream? Did he sleep at all?

My silent questions were interrupted by a phrase the priest said that has forever lodged into my head: "The slow and inefficient work of God."

He illustrated it with waves of the ocean, moment by moment moving in from the vast sea to land. In one wave, this motion does nothing. But slowly and inefficiently, whatever is in the ocean's way becomes worn smooth.

I thought back to the beaches down the road from me in California—the sand was smooth. The closer to the ocean I got, the smoother it got, until it felt as if I were walking on silk.

The slow and inefficient work of God.

I thought about the pew in front of me, worn and glassy from those who had rubbed past the gloss, through the stain, and worn the wood down to satin with their desperate fingers.

The slow and inefficient work of God.

I thought about my heart, rough and full of crag. The sharp

edges could pierce flesh, and I know have with misspoken words and irresponsible actions. I want God to change my heart. *Now.* I want him to take away my impatience, my entitlement to not feel lonely sometimes, the way I can impose on others. Take it away, God. *Now?*

He gently says no as a single wave of his grace washes over.

And then another.

I could move my heart further from the ocean and let it live untouched and unbothered by this seemingly unproductive task of rebuilding and the fearful task of being vulnerable. I could build a dam around it and not let the waters in. Or I could simply sit and let the waters of grace slowly, moment by moment, smooth my heart out. I could persevere.

We do not have to sit in green recliners and numb ourselves out in a world of pixels and stories we believe to be more exciting than our own. It is easy to find resolve in them because these stories resolve. Our stories have not yet resolved, and until we pass from this world into the next, they will not. We are still turning pages in the first act. The times when we are tempted to consider our failures as an end to an epic battle are instead the times when we must consider our failures to be the very things that launch us forward. We cannot dwell on them or dismiss them; we must pay them the respect they have earned and we must step forward, slowly as it may be. God does not demand progress or perfection from us. He simply calls us to believe.

When we believe, he will give us strength, even when we don't know it or how it will come. When I stepped (step by step by step) into vulnerability, those around me carried me into another season of growth and wonder, and that is where perseverance entered. I had to believe God was as tangible as I asked him to be, even when I did not recognize him. He showed his face in the silence, in the features of my friends, and even in the eyes of a Catholic priest from Tanzania.

Trust he is there and trust he will reveal himself to you as you persist. Ask. Knock. Seek. Wait. Embrace what comes: joy or pain. Remember that suffering produces perseverance; perseverance, character; and character, hope.[1] And it is that hope that will remain.

10

THE COLLISION OF
FAITH AND HOPE

Not only think of the road through which thou art traveling,
but take care never to lose sight of that blessed country in
which thou art shortly to arrive. Thou meetest here with
passing sufferings, but wilt soon enjoy everlasting rest. When
thou lookest up to the recompense everything thou dost or
sufferest will appear light, and no more than a shadow; it
bears no proportion with what thou art to receive for it. Thou
wilt wonder that so much is given for such trifling pains.

—SAINT AUGUSTINE

The year I was thirty was a year filled with grief and loss, betrayal and rejection in its most intimate form. Could I recover? The dust from dirt on the bottom of a well filled my lungs as I breathed in, maybe for the last time. I prepared for impact. Instead, a fight for liberation. Friends pulled me up with superhuman strength, fighting the forces of gravity and hopelessness.

I was pulled back into the sun; its brightness causing me to face the demons both within me and outside me. One by one, a brutal clashing. Victory was promised to me and I claimed it, but the battle-inflicted wounds were tender and my strength diminished.

The following year there were days of glorious beauty— with friends, with food, with wine, with music. Sunsets that inexplicably consumed my senses. Quiet walks where I begged God for nourishment. For plenty. For restoration of what was lost. Sometimes he did not answer with the abundance I thought I needed.

"Your daily bread is enough," was the response.

As the silence and the cover of grey clouds increased, I lost sight of the sunrises and the sunsets. The wind was colder and the moon hid behind veiled fog and my spirit drifted away, focusing on the wounds I could see instead of the mysteries I could not. Instead of roaming the paths under silver pine trees, my fingers roamed the damages in my heart. I followed them back to the more shadowy times and sat there, stubborn and unmoving.

It was winter, eight months since forming my team of intentional, vulnerable, and committed community. It was my second Christmas season alone. The choice before me wasn't clear, but I made the decision to put away the whiskey and the Coke and said good-bye to Don Draper, and I marched away from the shadows and determined to celebrate the season with joy, regardless of what my emotions spoke.

I went to Target and bought a small Christmas tree and a five-dollar bag of ornaments and a box of big globe-bulb lights. It was only a tree, and a borderline tacky one at that with its glittery pink star. But it was symbolic of my choice to embrace the Christmas music constantly barraging my eardrums and to embrace the season of anticipation that was before me in Advent.

I left Target. I was not praying. I was not pleading. I was not even thinking. The greats say mindfulness brings us closest to God, and I couldn't have been further from being mindful on this drive home.

And then, a collision: not between steel and plastic and fiberglass but between grace and the well in my heart. Something so large, so redeeming and indescribable ran me over on northbound I-65, and my heart's draw to the well was released.

Freedom exploded in my chest as I wept from a fount of joy and living water I had never tasted before. Crying was no surprise. In the days, weeks, months, years after my marriage ended, I cried more tears than I did in all of the thirty-something years of life before then.

These tears were different.

They were tears of joy.

Pure, crazy, maniacal, absurd, unexplainable tears of joy.

Hope ran over me like a semitruck. People were hope. Scripture was hope. My own potential was hope. Truth was hope. Church was hope. Love was hope. Strangers. Family. Food. Stars. Hiking. Cycling. Sun. Christmas trees. Cold air. Warm breezes. Colors. Embraces. Smiles. Coffee. Music. Friends. Laughter. Babies. Candles. Wine. Books.

An infinite explosion of subtleties and miracles filled me with hope.

Did grief still exist?

Yes.

Regret?

Yes.

Sadness?

Yes.

Confusion?

Yes.

Fear?

Yes.

Yes, yes, yes.

But now hope was visible. Hope was there! Hope walked around these broken places in my heart and gently touched each one, reminding me of their purpose.

I laughed and cried for a solid ten minutes, wondering if this was a lavish gift from God, full of life, and it was finally the day he chose to give it to me . . . or was I certifiably manic? I didn't care. I knew the truth would come with each sunrise.

I wasn't quite sure what I was supposed to do. Write? I worked on a poetry eBook. Speak? A few events came my way. Most of my time was spent back at Dose or setting up coffee dates with friends in downtown Franklin, trying to write, trying to figure out what the next thirty years of my life would look like. I looked for jobs but nothing ever manifested. I was still living in my two-room apartment that I avoided as much as possible. Living on my own was uncomfortable. Each time I walked into my tiny apartment with its mismatched thrift store furnishings, I was reminded again that this was not the way it was supposed to be.

I had almost daily talks with the Nashvillians on my team. They knew of my ups and downs while in Lincoln. They knew the . . . *stuckness* . . . I was feeling since I returned. They knew of my rediscovered hope and purpose.

What was the best way to steward this time I had?

One night as I sat in Michael and Gail's kitchen, I asked them what they thought about me going back to school.

"I think that's a fabulous idea," Gail responded.

"Really? Like, when I say 'go to school' I mean 'go away for school.' I need some fresh air away from Nashville." Earlier in the year when Liz suggested I move back and dig out the infection from my deepest wound, nobody knew what that looked like. As I talked about moving away for school, I knew it wasn't because I wanted to escape. The infection was gone. The scar remained but the cut was healed. It seemed counterintuitive to leave the community that had been my life support for almost the last year, but I felt that I needed to see if I could survive off life support; not alone, but breathing on my own again.

"Do you think I'm healthy enough to do that?" I asked, more questioning myself than Michael or Gail.

"I really do think you are, Anne," Michael said. "We've seen so much growth in you this last year, especially in these last few months. Feel it out, ask around, and if you have peace about it, I think it would be really good for you."

I was slightly shocked. Their affirmation of my growth and

my ability to make a healthy decision was strange to me. I felt equal parts twelve years old and thirty-one. Equal parts unsure and grown-up.

The next week, using the last free flight voucher I had, I flew to California. I wanted to visit the rest of my team and thank them and share the joy I had in a way that could only be communicated face-to-face.

After making my rounds in L.A. and Orange County, I drove down to San Diego to Bob's house. We hopped in his son's black truck and took a short drive to the Starbucks down the road. He caught me up on his family's adventures and I shared the school idea with him.

"Oh, absolutely. Fabulous. I'd just do one thing if I were you."

"What's that?"

"Commit to a year. Just one year. Regardless of where you go, go for the full year. Don't live anywhere else; don't move anywhere else, just dive in and give one full year your all."

"I think that's wise advice."

"The good thing about a year is if it doesn't work out, you know when it ends and you can move back to Nashville or choose to spend another year somewhere else. But if it does work out, you can stay. Either way, you win."

I took Bob's advice and Michael and Gail's support and started applying to a couple of schools—one on the East Coast and one in West Michigan. There was a small, Christian liberal arts school there (which donned quite the enchanting name: Hope College) that was half the tuition of the larger school I was considering on the East Coast. Although Holland wasn't very big, it was close to Grand Rapids and sat right on the beach front of Lake Michigan. The downtown was charming and reminded me a bit of Franklin. There was good coffee and fresh air. *I think this is it.*

It was only a couple of weeks before classes started when I applied, but miraculously, everything got processed and I was accepted. I got a grant I wasn't expecting, as well as a decent financial aid package. I had three weeks to pack up my tiny apartment and move to Holland, Michigan, where I committed to live in community and go to school for a year.

There was something about this move, this new expedition, that was just *right*. I couldn't explain it. I was sad to leave my friends in Nashville and a little scared since I only knew one person in Holland, but the doors to this new chapter blew open with fury and I couldn't resist its pull. Matt and my friend Brian helped me pack up the few boxes I had, I hooked up a small trailer to the back of my Toyota, and a few days before the New Year I made the drive up to Holland.

The Sunday before classes began, I went to Hope's bookstore, spent a ghastly amount of money on textbooks, and drove to a house where I rented a room. I took out the receipt from the bag and blindly tunneled my hand into my center console to find a pen. I dug around: my broken sunglasses, a napkin. I pulled out something that felt strange as I touched it. It was a rock. Bewildered, I turned it over in my hand and saw the handwritten scribble in Wite-Out that said "Hope," and I remembered the woman who gave it to me in Lincoln.

I couldn't help but grin. Hope found me, and I found hope.

I was even wearing a college hoodie that had "HOPE" written on it in big orange-and-blue letters. I was surrounded by hope. For so long, I wanted so desperately to hear from God in tangible ways—sure, he waited a long time, but now I felt as if I couldn't get him to stop, and this was more than fine by me.

Armed with the constant reminder that I was quite literally surrounded by hope, I was still concerned about how this idea of having a vulnerable, committed community would play out in a brand-new place with people I didn't even know. Of course, I still had my team on board, but what about the face-to-face time, the incarnational element that made the last year so rich? Because I saw the endless good that resulted from my choice to be intentional, vulnerable, and committed before, with those principles in mind, I walked out in faith, hoping they would stay true.

As an introvert, it was difficult to start the process of getting to know people, but over time, it became easier. I made a vow to say yes to everything I could in the beginning: cookouts, movie nights, and poetry readings at Hope where I knew I was the oldest student and even some of the professors were younger than me. As expected, some relationships stuck and developed; others didn't. I got to know the baristas at Lemonjello's, the coffee shop across the street from the school where I spent my time studying and reading and writing.

Soon, it was hard to go anywhere without running into someone. There were consistent girls' nights where we watched *So You Think You Can Dance* and ate handfuls of whatever fruit was in season at the local orchards. On Tuesday nights, friends and strangers would bring whatever food we could and ate dinner on blankets and picnic tables (which I found familiar, as I knew my Nashville team was communing on the same evening). After a few months, I realized the committed part of my relationships manifested. There were people in Holland I saw and met with regularly.

For these relationships to blossom into life-giving and life-receiving ones, I knew the next step would be allowing myself to be more vulnerable. Most of these friends knew the basics of my story, but what about now? What about the things I wrestled with?

Anxiety has always been one of my greatest battles. Irrational fears and worries started running after me when I was fourteen, and throughout the years, I have been on and off medication for it. Though it's managed well, depending on my stress level, it can still fly off the charts. At the end of the spring semester, I noticed the increase of racing thoughts, the consistently elevated heart rate, and my lack of sleep. I was stressed because of finals, because of money, and because I began dating someone: a tall, blue-eyed Ohio native, Adam. He lived a few hours away from me, so the process of getting to know him only happened on weekends. After the first few weeks of our relationship, I realized we were not a match—not even close. In hindsight, I find it almost humorous that one of our greatest disconnects was how we viewed relationships with other people and community.

He didn't see a need to ask anyone, ever, for advice or counsel. When he learned about my team, he told me in no uncertain terms that he saw me as their puppet and questioned my ability to make decisions for myself. After that conversation, I knew our brief relationship needed to end, but breaking up was something I didn't have much experience doing. I asked Adam if we could spend a couple of weeks without visiting each other to think about things. He didn't understand why the value of community was so important to me, even after hearing my story, but he agreed to give me some space.

As I was sitting on the patio of Lemonjello's between classes with a mug of coffee, I sent a text message to Gail and Shelia, asking for their prayers for my anxiety about school and Adam. I scrolled through my contacts and sent the same text to Christen, a friend I was getting to know in Holland. She happened to walk by pushing her one-year-old son Sam in a stroller just a few minutes later and asked if I wanted to talk about it. I opened up to her about my nervousness with finals—and about the relationship with Adam. In turn, she shared some of her own struggles with anxiety with me. She asked if we could pray together. I said yes, and over a wobbly aluminum table on the corner of Ninth and College Streets, we prayed.

This was a shift, and one I wasn't expecting to happen. My team in Nashville (and California and Virginia) was still intact, but I found myself in an equally committed and vulnerable friendship—one that didn't take much time to form. I realized the principles held true. Time, location, age, status—none of that really mattered as long as I was willing to engage *and* be engaging with others.

And I realized something new: this was no longer a one-way street. I wanted to give back the love and sacrifice others gave me by being a safe place for me to be me.

Christen lived four blocks down the road from me and it was easy to pop over for tea at night. She and her husband, Tony, would invite small groups of people over for prayer nights where we'd sing and pray and share. Sometimes, she'd need someone to watch Sam for a couple of hours while Tony was at work so she could run an errand. We went to a poetry reading in Grand Rapids and would enjoy a glass of wine at Butch's as we watched people wander on Eighth Street, window-shopping. When I spoke at a local church, she magically wrangled a baby-sitter for Sam and snuck in a few minutes late. Just seeing her face in a crowd of mostly strangers gave me confidence as I spoke. We celebrated and prayed together. We read and talked about relationships. When threatening moments started forcing their way into my mind (or hers), we knew there was another person nearby to help carry the other.

Finals came and went without much trouble. I prepared well and passed. My parents in Texas received a certificate on my behalf for making it on the Dean's List, which they found terrific and put up on their refrigerator. I found it hilarious considering I was paying my own way. As a reward for finishing my first semester as a full-time student, I decided to spend a week in Nashville for a conference. I stayed with Michael and Gail, and after dinner at a wine bar down the street, they asked how I was doing with processing my relationship with Adam. I laid out my nervousness about ending the relationship, even though it was only a few weeks old and I knew it needed to end. Outside of sharing the same beliefs about God, Adam and I simply didn't share the same values on money, on roles in a relationship, on social issues, on politics, or on the big one—community. The last thing I wanted to do was hurt someone, but I really didn't see another option.

Just to eliminate any hesitations I had, Michael bluntly asked me, "What does your gut say?"

"It says I should end it."

"Well, then, you know what to do."

The next day, I called Adam and let him know the relationship was over. Over the phone may not have been the best way to handle the situation, but I didn't see it prudent to make a trip to Ohio to do it face-to-face. Maybe it was fear; maybe it was wisdom. Regardless, I soon felt the freedom—and confidence—of knowing that, with help, I made several good decisions: I asked for prayer when I noticed the first signs of trouble; I opened up to good friends for their wisdom; and I took action.

Earlier, I compared seasons of joy and pain to the rotation of the earth; sometimes our skies are starless and other times we marvel at the colors in the landslide[1] of clouds at dusk. Sorrowful seasons end and joy always finds us.

If I plotted on a story line the events of my life between the summer following my thirtieth birthday and this moment, the drive home after purchasing that cheap Christmas tree was the climax. It was a distinct, pivotal point in my journey where really, at the risk of sounding cliché, everything changed. While life after this pinnacle moment does not and will never resemble anything flawless, and even while many circumstances remain the same, my perspective was forever altered. My periphery expanded, and I realized I not only survived but was strong.

This strength wasn't because of anything I held; instead, as I extracted my fingers from the scars and the silhouettes of grief, they began exploring the new web of life around me—a web made of millions of tiny moments and prayers and embraces and words and nothing and everything in between. My team and others who walked alongside me stitched in a thread here and a thread there until I was completely sewn into a brilliant world where I could walk again and breathe again and give again. I finally felt healthy. Like an adult again. The conference ended, I drove back to Holland, and I was excited to spend the summer with my friends on the lake, catch up on some reading and a new hobby, write letters, and explore whatever the next right step would be.

11

RECEIVING AND RETURNING

*In Heaven there will be no anguish and no duty of turning
away from our earthly Beloveds. First, because we shall
have turned already; from the portraits to the Original,
from the rivulets to the Fountain, from the creatures He
made loveable to Love Himself. But secondly, because
we shall find them all in Him. By loving Him more than
them we shall love them more than we now do.*

—C. S. LEWIS, *THE FOUR LOVES*

ack in Holland, after the conference and back to being
cheerfully single, I determined my full-time job for the
month of May was reading. I would not feel guilty about spending
the day with coffee and muffins and the sun and a book. Because
of a small grant I received, I had this luxury for a short time, and
it was one I was not going to let slip away. In June, I started writing
again, a biweekly column for a magazine. This rhythm helped me
refind and refine my voice with purpose and a deadline.

In July, a tragedy struck. My friend Jay, one of my cycling teammates from the cross-country tour I participated in a few summers prior, was in a fatal accident. Most of the cycling team flew from our scattered hometowns to Georgia for his funeral. Jay was one of the bravest and most compassionate people I've ever met. The tiny community of Plains, Georgia, including Jimmy Carter's wife, gathered in the sticky heat to celebrate his life. Something about Jay's passing reminded me of how fragile my own time was and how urgently I needed to love others because *I had been loved first*.[1] Jay did not procrastinate love. He copiously poured it on everybody he met. There was a new focus within me: intentionally love, regardless.

In August, I took a trip to Africa to visit my friends Melissa and Jim, who are missionaries. They live in Swaziland, a South African country unfortunately known for its gruesome AIDS statistics rather than its grandiose mountain landscapes, warm hearts, and flawless starry nights. Swazis are forgotten people in a forgotten country, and the more removed someone is from the capital city of Mbabane, the more forgotten they become.

Melissa was also on the cycling team with Jay and me, and I brought a copy of Jay's funeral program for her. We remembered Jay and told stories about the crazy ways he sacrificially loved us on the team—from carrying an extra milk jug of water just in case someone needed it, to pushing a struggling teammate twice his size up a mountain.

During my last weekend in Africa, we drove across the country from Hawane to Lavumisa, one of the most remote rural villages on the southeast side of the country. The sun did not sympathize with the winter season. What should have been alive was dead, and the only green we saw was sewn into the fabric wraps women wore around their midsections as they carried their babies along the dirt road. Three of us walked in a dusty heat from the footbridge across a dry riverbed to Lindiwe's homestead at the edge of the village.

At a church service the night before, my missionary friends, Melissa and Jim, had learned about Lindiwe from a local nurse named Lisa. Lindiwe developed breast cancer two years ago, and as the country's standard treatment offered, she had a mastectomy on her right side. There is no chemotherapy or radiation available in Swaziland. Nobody can afford it; therefore the hospitals don't offer it.

Lindiwe is a traditional Swaziland mother who lives in a stick-and-stone mud hut with a thatch roof. Most of her family lives around her in similar structures, but only one was inside her home when we arrived. Instead of sleeping on the customary bed of a rolled bamboo mat and a wooden headrest, someone had brought a six-inch-thick plastic mattress in for Lindiwe. Melissa, Jim and I, now accompanied by Lisa, another missionary, and a translator entered the hut and announced our visit in Siswati: "*Ekaye!*" To which she replied in English, "Come in."

We crawled in the shortened opening and sat on the floor, filling up most of Lindiwe's hut. Our translator asked how she was feeling and described to us how bad Lindiwe said her pain was. Her ankles were swollen and her arms full of lymphatic fluid. Because of the swelling, she couldn't rest. Lisa checked her medicines to see if it was possible to increase them. She could. *Grace.* Hopefully that would provide a little more relief so Lindiwe could sleep.

Lindiwe's daughter sat beside her silently, her face somber and her eyes never leaving the smoothed dirt floor. We took turns reading Scripture to Lindiwe and praying and asking careful questions. *How long had it been since she slept through the night? Did she have enough food? Were the pain medicines working?*

As our visit came to a close, Lindiwe abruptly interrupted our translator, who paused before telling us what she had said.

"It's not so much the physical pain she is suffering from," the translator said. "It's the loneliness."

I commanded my eyes to remain dry, but my breath got lost in my lungs for a moment. In the last six years, I've witnessed physical pain and poverty. I've seen children in Uganda without clothes and with bellies empty but distended, full of worms and disease. I've seen homeless men with infected wounds in Los Angeles. In India, I visited Mother Teresa's Home for the Dying and wept as I stepped over frail bodies waiting on the staircase for a bed. My heart broke in Haiti a month after the earthquake as a woman named Michele told the story of her house collapsing on her, immediately killing her eighteen-month-old twins and crushing her legs. Her husband's cries of grief would make almost anyone question God and humanity. I've seen the loss of homes and loved ones in Louisiana, Oklahoma, Colorado, and Tennessee; tragedy does not discriminate.

Yet tragic is an understated descriptor of all of these experiences. As Lindiwe openly shared, it's the wound loneliness leaves that often causes the most ache. Is feeling alone and forgotten worse than physical pain?

When I sat in Lindiwe's home in Swaziland, words and prayers didn't seem adequate. I walked away with hot tears inside my eyes, still stubbornly refusing to fall. It's tempting to feel guilt for leaving when I could have stayed. Sure, my flight was the next day, but it's just an airplane. There will always be more flights back to the United States. I could change my plans and remain in Swaziland for just a few more days, or weeks, or months. But I didn't stay. Melissa and Jim drove me to Johannesburg the next day, and I was back home two days later.

Does thirty minutes really show love to a woman in such a painful place? Does three weeks? Three months? Three years? How much time does love need to matter? In Africa or in Michigan? These questions, for me anyway, have not been answered. But as a friend says, sometimes questions are more important than the answers.

In the beginning, when Gail called me early that Wednesday morning in Florida, when I was in the hotel room afraid and despairing, she asked me without hesitation in her voice to move in with them until I was ready to move out. She didn't know what it would look like. Would it be enough to help or would it maybe be too much? She did not overthink love. She simply entered in. This was love. This was hospitality. This was right.

Michael and Gail knew I had little to offer when I arrived. I couldn't pay them any money to help with the astronomical electric bill that arrived each month to cool their house from the harsh Tennessee heat, or even promise to be an easy houseguest.

They knew they would need to carry me for a while, both materially and emotionally. Except for baking an endless number of cookies each week—a kind of therapy for me—I really had nothing to give them in return.

They did not expect repayment. I was not used to this generosity or hospitality or care; not without giving back. I battled between feeling overwhelmed with gratefulness and overwhelmed with guilt. I did not see myself worthy to be served like this, so unconditionally.

It reminded me of spending Holy Week with Susan. On Maundy Thursday, I joined her for the service. The bishop used the passage where Simon Peter refuses to let Jesus wash his feet, and Jesus's response to him.

PETER: "You will not wash my feet, now or ever!"

JESUS: "If I don't wash you, you will have nothing to do with Me."[2]

Simon Peter had a point, and I'd probably have the same reaction. "Sorry, Jesus. You're, you know . . . *Jesus* . . . and I am not going to let you wash my feet." He felt unworthy to have his leader, someone he knew was the Messiah, get down and clean his dirty feet.

How often do we feel the same way?

How often do we not want to let people in (or Jesus for that matter) because we feel we are burdening them with our dirty feet?

As I sat in the pew next to Susan, stuck, I felt like a walking weight. I didn't feel worthy enough to be carried. And so much of the shame and guilt from my past kept God's all-restoring, all-perfecting love at arm's length.

No, Jesus, you can't wash my feet.

I'm too . . .

Broken.

Hopeless.

Confused.

Aimless.

You should have given up on me by now.

"Let me wash your feet."

But . . .

"Let me wash your feet. If you desire me, you will let me wash your feet."

The church leaders up front pulled out bowls and water.

What?

We were going to have a foot-washing ceremony, in church?

But there are so many of us.

This is going to take forever.

Where am I supposed to put my shoes?

What?

Wash my feet?

No.

No.

No.

"Go, Anne. Go."

I know God's voice when I hear it.

I made my way to the front.

I pulled my red shoes off and tucked my socks inside. I sat in a chair and waited. Finally, I walked to the bowl and sat down in front of it.

The junior bishop dipped his towel into the bowl as I placed my feet in it. He said a prayer of blessing over me, thanking God for the "path he has placed me on." Interesting. If only he knew my path, maybe he wouldn't say such crazy things. Or maybe he does know somehow? Who knows? Another leader dried my feet off. I walked back to my shoes, picked them up, and made my way back to my seat. I placed my arms on the pew in front of me and laid my head in them.

Why do you still love me? How can anyone still love me? I feel so helpless.

I continued pushing away the love that was trying to envelop me, to be lavished on me.

No . . . no . . . no . . . you can't wash my feet.

"I already did . . ."

As the choir sang and the rest of the congregation had their feet washed, I realized how hard it is for me to choose to receive love, and learning to receive love is just as important as giving it.

I am glad I learned this lesson so close to the time I found myself living with Michael and Gail. It was not easy to meet their generosity and say that I needed it. On one hand, it was such mercy to have a beautiful home with beautiful souls in it to rest in, to pray in, to live in, to eat in. I did not take one of those days for granted, and even now my body is warmed remembering each of them. However, the choice to receive this, to be humbled and to realize I am only made up of the breath, the blood, the Spirit. And the Spirit within the people God supplies me—freely at that—rebels against everything in my strong-willed bones.

If we allow it, everything we experience comes full circle here on earth as it is in heaven . . . if we allow it. I moved out on my own when I was seventeen years old and have always been able to provide for myself. So being provided for by another family now was difficult to accept. But in the breaking of my thick ego, I learned a most holy lesson about generosity and how everything we think we own is only ours to be stewarded.

Darrell Vesterfelt once stated, "We can't give gifts we haven't received first."[3]

Jesus knew his disciples would not be able to love with his love unless they could receive it. I believe that in the moment when he washed their feet, Peter finally understood it as well. He went from protesting to responsive, even asking for more.

> Then wash me but don't stop with my feet. Cleanse my hands and head as well![4]

Love is a concept too infinite for my finite understanding. Knowing I will not ever know the correct answer provides me room to freeze with fear or move forward with faith. I choose faith, and it says to *go, love, and believe.* Enter in where there is pain and love. Do not worry about if it's enough. Believe it is enough for the moment.

12

SAFE PLACES

It takes a lot of strength and patience for one to invest time and effort in rebuilding ruins. But it's another chance for rebirth.

—FRANK MATOBO

Two days after I returned from Africa and two days before classes started back up at Hope, I was half-asleep on my couch, staring into my television, trying to stay awake just long enough to push through the jet lag. I opened my computer for the first time in several weeks and a list of e-mails dropped in from my month away.

In it, an unexpected note from a Christian dating site. Back in the spring, I started to write a research paper on how online dating was creating false intimacy in one of the most cherished, incarnational, and sacred relationships a person can have. I signed up for three sites, filled out the profiles with a note at the bottom of each stating (boldly), "I doubt I will meet anyone online. Part of me just finds it creepy."

As it turns out, that's how I met Adam, the man from Ohio, which further proved my point. The process of seeing most eligible bachelors taking a picture of themselves in the mirror as their main photo, followed by a picture of them at a bar or party with a red plastic cup, followed by a picture of them with a cute niece, followed by a picture of them with some kind of fast motor vehicle, and lastly a picture of them posing with a dead rabbit/deer/fish began to wear on me. Two of my three dating accounts expired, and the third I took offline. I changed the topic of my paper.

Evidently, however long my profile was hidden was just long enough that the third site reminded me of all the great potential matches who were just waiting for me to reactivate my account. It wouldn't cost anything. Just look. See who's new. *For free!*

I blamed the jet lag for lowering my defenses and I clicked on the link. I scrolled through a few generic photographs before landing on one that was quite a bit different. In it, you couldn't even really make out what the guy looked like because he was surrounded by a group of kids and was clearly on a mission trip. I glanced to the right of the screen where his location was listed. Illinois. *Hmm. Probably Chicago.* That's only two hours from me. Appears to be a mission trip guy. He's close. Why not? I clicked.

He wrote about how he was passionate about adoption and orphans and how he went through a terrible divorce but believes marriage is for life. He was in the arts and performed improv on the side. He wanted to fight a bear before he died and have an action figure made of him. I clicked through his other two pictures so I could get a better sense of what he looked like. No mirror photos. No dead animals. Dark brown eyes. Friendly face . . .

A couple of months had passed since he last signed on to the dating site, so my best guess was that he probably wouldn't respond. Maybe he met someone or perhaps the online dating thing repulsed him as it did me. When I was still doing research for my paper, I also searched and saw what single girls were putting on their profiles. It wasn't much better than what most guys offered.

I decided to message him.

Hey there,

I don't ever send these messages, really. I actually signed up originally because I was researching for a sociology paper—not because I wanted to date. But I'm sure everyone says that.

Anyway, your profile was refreshing and we both have traveled to a lot of the same countries for a lot of the same reasons. If by chance you get this and are able to reply, it would be good to hear from you. If not, that's okay. I may even take my account down before you get this. I guess what's meant to happen will happen.

Take care,

AJ

I kept my account online until the day before classes started. That night, I checked from my phone and saw he read the message that day but didn't reply. *Whatever, Chicago Guy. I don't need you anyway.* I went to bed and planned to hide my profile again the next morning.

The next morning I woke up, made some juice, and turned my computer on. I checked my e-mail. *A new message is waiting for you.* Was it from Chicago Guy? Oh, fine. I'll log in just one more time.

The message was, in fact, from Chicago Guy. Except he wasn't *Chicago* Guy. He was Tim and he lived three hours west of Chicago in the Quad Cities/Davenport area. I mapped the route. *Five hours? Sheesh.* His reply was short and funny. After he proved he wasn't a crazy person (as much as one can through messaging), I gave him one of my e-mail addresses (in the event he was crazy). He now had my name and I knew that meant he could do a little online stalking if he wanted. As soon as he confirmed he had my e-mail address, I removed my profile from the dating site.

The next morning as I walked into a class where I was a teaching assistant, I fetched my e-mail through my phone. Tim had written. His snarky subject line caused me to laugh out loud in front of the students I'd soon be helping. *Gee, thanks.* I smiled. Something inside my heart flickered.

We began corresponding over e-mail for a few days, and the e-mails soon turned to phone calls. He made his intent very clear. He doesn't *date*. He wanted to court a girl with the possibility of marriage in mind from the beginning. Laugh all you want about *I Kissed Dating Goodbye*, but there was something attractive to me about good, old-fashioned courtship. There was nothing casual to his approach. He was looking for a partner in ministry and in life. Before we corresponded very long, he asked if I was healthy and ready to date after my divorce. I remembered what Matt told me once in our conversations about dating again after divorce. He knew me well: "You're healthy enough to date as long as the relationship is not a detriment to your health," was Matt's wise reply, and he helped me see any relationship is only as healthy as each person is.

Our conversations went late into the night. After a few weeks, he asked if he could visit me in Holland. I timidly said yes, still fully determined to remain single and enjoy the freedom it brought, but slightly intrigued by how different Tim was in his philosophy of relationships and community and his passion for loving others. And if he was using an online dating site, surely there was something tragically wrong with him.

"How should I greet you when I meet you?" he asked on the phone the night before our first date. "Should I give you a hug? A handshake? Should I throw a rock through your neighbor's window?"

Out of nowhere, I gave him a list of whatever random things flowed into my stream of consciousness.

"Well, first pull up in the vacant lot across from my house. You'll have flowers, of course. I'd also like some balloons but no yellow ones. I don't like yellow. After the balloons, a bird release of some kind would be nice and while this is all happening, if you could get the Hope College marching band to play behind you while fireworks are going off, I think that'd work."

The next day, I got sporadic updates through text messages from Tim about his whereabouts. One picture he sent was full of lush trees and "U-Pick" Michigan farm billboards and I recognized the spot—about half an hour away. Because my doorbell didn't work, I walked downstairs to unlock the front door so he could just come in when he arrived. When I pulled the door open, I saw his car across the street from my house. *Sneaky.*

I tiptoed back inside and sent him a text message. "Busted." I saw him read the text from my living room window and went outside to meet him.

Holy moly. He is really, really cute. Tim was wrestling some balloons in the lakeshore wind while he reached in the car to get flowers.

"Hi," he said, handing me both the flowers and the balloons—no yellow.

"I thought you were further out?" I teased.

He said nothing and reached into his backseat. He turned around to me and simply said, "Here are your dumb birds." A dozen or so rubber ducks went bouncing on Central Avenue around my feet as I held the flowers and the balloons. His eyes sparkled. We both laughed. He turned back to his car again.

"I couldn't find fireworks or a marching band, so I got you these streamers instead," he said as he handed me three rolls of paper streamers. He pulled out his phone and said, "I have a marching band pulled up on YouTube for you. Hope College doesn't have a marching band. Nice try."

I'm sure we were a sight to take in, me with my balloons whipping around and flowers and bright yellow rubber ducks around my feet. We went back inside my house where I put the flowers in a vase, and from there we proceeded to have the most fun first date, getting incredibly lost for hours in a corn maze on a farm on the outskirts of Grand Rapids. We found our way out only by listening to the bullhorn telling us it was closing time and the last ride back to the parking lot was about to leave. Second graders completed the maze faster than we did.

The rest of Tim's first visit was very fun and very real, all at the same time. I couldn't believe how laid back and honest he was and how he opened every door for me every time. His heart for community and genuine relationships beat in the same rhythm as mine. I knew I was healthy enough to be in a relationship again, but did I want to be?

After a couple of months and many visits back and forth to see each other, one night we were out at one of his improv events. He had "the boys"—three high school students he mentored, Kristoffer, James, and Wes—sneak into the house where I was staying. The entire time Tim and I knew each other, he was taking notes on my favorite things—music, cupcakes, tea, fruit, anything that sparkles—and he had the boys set up an indoor picnic that included them all. We walked into the dreamland of twinkle lights and flowers he created and I knew he heard me, he listened. *I knew he knew me.* He started the playlist he made of all the artists I ever mentioned to him. The first song to come on was one I played on repeat since those dark, dark days years before. He had no idea the weight the lyrics of this song carried when he planned for it to be the first one to play.

> *I feel the light upon my skin,*
> *Like finger-tips*
> *Reminding me that night must end.*

Be brave
Like bridges underwater,
Keeping strong beyond their time.
I feel the light upon my skin,
Reminding me that night must end.

There's something about sadness
that leaves us wanting more
A sickness that breathes . . .
From holding on to letting go,
The change is like dying.

Be brave
Like bridges underwater,
Keeping strong beyond their time.
Feel the light upon your skin,
Reminding you that night must end.

Teach me to create
A beautiful past
That makes you proud.
That makes you proud.

Teach me what I need to know
To be strong enough to let go . . .

Teach me what I need to know
To be strong enough to let go.[1]

I rested my head on his chest as I took it all in. I heard Someone whisper in my heart in a voice that was unmistakable and I knew I could let go.

You are in a safe place. You can trust your heart with him.

So I did.

I let go and jumped in and shared my joy of this new relationship with my team. I told them how we met, how I was afraid, how he treated me, how he treated others. How when I would speak somewhere he would somehow find out where I was staying and have flowers waiting in my hotel room for me. Nobody had any hesitation, though some of the southerners let him know they owned guns and were not afraid to use them if he hurt me.

As we each drove around Lake Michigan to visit the other, we became more and more enmeshed into each other's communities. Not only would I visit Tim when I'd drive to the Quad Cities, but there would be a girls' night out planned, a double date with another couple, lunch after church, and game nights with his friends. These small moments were the soil where deeper relationships grew, with Tim and with those who surrounded him. When he came to Holland, he got to know my friends and would scheme up surprises with them. Once, he connected with my friend, also named Tim, and asked if he could come to Holland . . . without me knowing about it. He needed a place to stay. Tim-the-friend said yes, and the next morning when I went into Lemonjello's for coffee before my first class, I saw *my* Tim sitting at the bar in the window, pretending to read a newspaper. My heart caught fire with electricity and love.

There was always some type of gathering where our circles

would crash together in such a lovely way. Not only was our relationship with each other growing, the roots of it, planted in healthy soil where they could grow, reached out and in and pulled in those we cherished most. Life from each one was funneled in, causing us to blossom. We reciprocated as our relationship breathed life back into the air, into raindrops that would soak into the soil, back to nourish the roots. Talks about marriage and the future entered our conversations. Would he move to Holland? Would I move to the Quad Cities? Would we just move somewhere else? Nashville? Texas? Where? In all of the places we considered, we knew as long as we kept putting effort into it, we'd be able to continue walking in the intricate and grace-filled opportunities for the kind of community both of us desperately knew we needed and wanted.

The holidays were approaching and we made plans to meet each other's families. I met his over Thanksgiving, and over Christmas, he met mine. We went to Texas via Nashville to spend some time with the group of friends who are considered nothing less than family. I arrived at Michael and Gail's the night before he did and went upstairs to the guest room he'd be sleeping in to make up his bed. It was the same room I stayed in two years before when I had nowhere else to go.

I was making up this same bed in the same room for a man I loved so deeply with a heart that was filled with so much joy. In one room, I was standing in two universes, one from my past and one in my present. Tim arrived and we celebrated Christmas with so many friends from Nashville, friends on the team, and friends I held just as dear. A small dinner party turned into a large feast as more and more showed up to meet this man who broke through my very guarded heart.

After a few days, Tim carried our luggage to my car and as he slipped out of earshot, Gail pounded her fist like a judge's gavel on the countertop in the kitchen.

"Approved, Anne. Approved." Gail's smile was wide and her eyes lit up bright.

Michael came out to the commotion and joined in.

"This is so good for you. *So good.* We are so excited for the both of you and to see where this leads. You don't need our blessing, but you have it anyway."

I smiled. Again, I was caught in separate worlds, recalling conversations of loss spoken over the same kitchen counter and now hearing such affirmation from those I trusted most about this brand-new season.

Christmas with my family was what Christmas looks like for most families: slightly chaotic, burning dinner, fights with siblings, but overall a covering of love and grace and a newfound acceptance.

With the blessing of those around us, Tim and I continued walking into our future. I moved to the quiet city of Moline, Illinois, close to where Tim lived. Saying good-bye to my friends in Holland was not an easy task. How could this once foreign city become a place where I belonged in such a short amount of time? I made a list of people to spend time with before I left and I realized it would be nearly impossible. Even saying good-bye to the staff at Lemonjello's was difficult. I bought a couple of pounds of coffee just so I could take the way it smelled and tasted with me. I remembered the times I spent staring out the window at the trees in front of Pillar Church writing articles or reading or doing homework.

Tim and his friend Chris drove up from the Quad Cities to help me load my U-Haul and make the trek. A crew of friends showed up to load everything in. I took them out to dinner at New Holland Brewery where more friends trickled in to say good-bye. We went to sleep that night on air mattresses scattered through the house. I gazed out my living room window, now barren of its green curtains, and looked at the empty lot across the street where I first saw Tim. My whole life was changing again and although I was sad to leave Holland, I was excited to continue leaning into my relationship with Tim.

Chris and Tim drove the U-haul away and I stayed back to clean out forgotten corners and closets and turn in my keys to the interesting Greek landlord who owned the house. I locked the door one last time and walked over to my car. In my driver's seat was a mug from Lemonjello's and a type-written note from my kindred friend Christen:

Anne,

You are leaving and I think I have tried to balance the "grief" with so much gratitude for how God surprised me with your authentic, accepting, joy-filled, raw friendship in my life during a season I was longing for authentic friendship. You were evidence that God cares about the details of our everyday lives. I'm excited to see the ways our friendship continues to grow over the months and years to come.

It's hard to say good-bye because there is so much joy and such life to our daily life here. I'm so thankful that we could find time between blow-out diapers (Sam adores you!), the need to withdraw, a desire to dream again and to be healed by God.

When I look back at this season in Holland I will remember kitchen conversations and heart-to-hearts where I was refreshed by the Spirit of the Living God flowing through you. Thank you for taking the time to get to know me . . . and love me. I'm so excited for you—and Tim!!!

I hope you will know that you will be deeply missed by me, Tony, and this community. (And Sam of course).

Love you and praying for you—by grace alone,

Christen

How could I leave this? I sat in my car for almost fifteen minutes wiping tears of sadness mingled with tears of joy from under my jaw as they rolled down to my shirt. I don't know how Christen broke into my car to plant the letter or the Lemonjello's mug, but she did. And I don't know how she managed to break into my small daily life in Holland, Michigan, where I wanted to live just for a year and test to see if God was faithful to me in relationships if I remained faithful to him and the things he taught me.

I thought a year of school, a few fun friends, and some stories about sunsets on Lake Michigan were what that season had in store for me, and I was perfectly content with that. But as Scripture says, he did more than I could have ever asked for or imagined. With Christen, he divinely knit together two spirits that would remain forever friends.

....

The drive to Moline was all too short as I tried hanging on to each mile and each moment of friendship and joy, afraid to surrender them, afraid they would be forgotten. But on arriving, a group of new friends was already in place to help us unload into a boxy apartment reminiscent of the 1970s, complete with a chocolate brown stove and an avocado green sink. All over my kitchen counters were flowers and baskets full of food and chocolate and a bottle of wine. Tim hung a huge welcome banner across the yellowed curtains in the kitchen windows. I was home. Again.

13

CIRCLES OR SPIRALS

*No kind of action ever stops with itself. One kind action
leads to another. Good example is followed. A single act of
kindness throws out roots in all directions, and the roots spring
up and make new trees. The greatest work that kindness
does to others is that it makes them kind themselves.*

—AMELIA EARHART

As I leaned over my computer on my kitchen table, I got an e-mail from Tim. He forwarded me a message from Natalie, a youth leader he served with at church. She asked if the "Anne Jackson" he was dating was the "same Anne Jackson who struggled with Internet pornography in her teens." Tim knew my story, and wrote back to Natalie and said I was. He put the two of us in touch and she sent me an e-mail asking if I'd be willing to meet with her daughter, Rachel.

Rachel was a senior in high school and had lived a rough few years: her parents' divorce, sexual abuse at the hands of a trusted family friend when she was in elementary school, and for the last six years of her life, an addiction to Internet pornography. She kept it a secret for most of that time, just recently confessing to Natalie everything that happened. She wanted freedom and she saw no way out.

I met with Rachel at the café in a university bookstore. She arrived before I did and had a stack of familiar Christian books on healthy sexuality and a journal. She leaned against the wall looking as though she'd rather be anywhere else but there.

I waved quietly to catch her attention since she didn't know what I looked like, and she sat up. I walked halfway over to her table, just close enough where she could hear me, and asked if I could buy her a coffee or tea. She said no, and I ordered a cookie and a dark roast for me.

I sat down across from her and noted how weird it was we were meeting in such a public place to talk about such an awkward subject. She looked down, her brown hair covering her blushing face, and nodded.

"I really don't know how to do this," I confessed. "I know your mom wanted us to meet because our stories are similar, but I want to make sure this 'meeting'"—I made air quotes—"is something you really want to do."

She remained quiet.

"Would you like for me to share my story with you? Or do you want to share yours with me? I really don't know how these things work," I laughed, poorly disguising my nerves.

Rachel hesitated a moment and asked me to share mine.

For the next fifteen minutes or so, I gave her the highlight-reel version of my life: I was the good preacher's girl who left the church after the church hurt my family; the youth pastor who paid attention to me when I was at my loneliest and how he abused that vulnerability when he molested me my junior year in high school; how I started looking at pornography on the Internet at about the same time and how I couldn't stop for eons; the shame that came with that and my many attempts to quit on my own.

I told her about one of the most significant moments in my battle with pornography. When I was twenty-one, five years after the sexual abuse and the beginning of me looking at porn online, I met a girl named Kristi who opened up to me about her own struggles with pornography and lust, and for the first time in five years, I professed my own wrongs and desire for freedom. I shared how Kristi gave me a gift by going first. It's always hard to go first but because she did, she gave me the gift of going second, when it's just a little easier. After years of friendship and accountability, removing the Internet from my house, not having cable, addressing the real reason *why* I was looking at pornography to begin with, and desiring God's best for me, I was healthy. I was free. I wasn't perfect. I still slipped up now and again. Those times are few and far between and the sorrow that comes with each moment grieves me deeper and deeper. Overall, the burden of carrying the compulsion to look and lust was gone. Freedom was possible.

I didn't expect Rachel to say much back. She was extremely shy and rarely made eye contact with me when I told her about my journey. I felt awful for her, not knowing what to say or do to help because sometimes there is nothing you can say or do. She played with the string that tied her journal together and in time, told me her story, much of which I knew from her mom, but I soaked in each of her words as if I had never heard them before, empathizing with most of them.

She told me on the following Wednesday she was going to a retreat center in Indiana, a place that focused on helping women find wholeness and healing from pornography. She said she hadn't looked at porn for two days—the longest she's gone in a long, long time—and she felt sick. She was shaking. She couldn't eat. Her anxiety was through the roof. I told her I'd pray for her daily while she was at the retreat and maybe we could catch up when she was home and ready to talk about her experience in Indiana.

She texted me a few times as she traveled to the retreat center, but when she arrived they confiscated her phone. I didn't hear from her for an entire week, but when she reemerged, she was full of hope. It was difficult, she said, but she felt completely equipped to handle it.

Rachel and I met up at a Starbucks by her school. She was doing great and it was almost three weeks without looking at pornography. She didn't have access to it most of the time, which helped, but she could feel her mind and heart embrace the new creation she learned she was. I may have started out as a mentor to her, but we became friends.

Even though Rachel is almost half my age, we can connect. We both desire the same openness and honesty in relationships. Though I won't be able to relate to her in many ways because of our age difference, and she can't relate to the things I'm learning at this phase in my life, every time we get together—whether we're talking about spiritual things or just getting our toenails painted at the mall—my heart is full of joy knowing God has done such a work in me that I can now live out of his abundance and pour into others. And as Rachel continues getting healthier, it's a beautiful and sacred gift to see her pour into a group of junior-high girls she leads at her church.

One of the things that drew me to Tim was how he shared the desire to disciple younger men. Tim grew up with very broken family dynamics; his dad was a weekend dad who showed him love by giving him things. Without a father figure around, Tim wasn't sure how to navigate growing into adulthood. When he hit thirty, after returning to the same unhealthy habits over and over again, God gave him relief and the responsibility to help teenage guys and young adults learn some of the things he learned and hopefully save them a few scars along the way.

Over the last few years, the three students Tim has mentored during their high school years, the same ones who set up that special night for me, have met and struggled and been honest with each other. We recently attended their graduation, and as they walked down the aisle to the stage and saw Tim, you could see just *how* excited they were that he was there. First James, then Kristoffer, and then Wes. Each one walked across the stage and moved his tassel from the right to the left.

Kristoffer decided to study abroad in Europe for a year, James is going with him for a while, and Wes is getting his first apartment. These boys are now men. On a warm Monday afternoon, Tim and I were invited to Kristoffer's house and we walked into a dining room with folded napkins and the best china and silverware placed in all the right places. Sparkling grape juice was poured. They served us a meal thoughtfully crafted, and there was no detail missed, from the small fruit dishes to the pitcher of water, which since the day my feet were washed at Susan's church always reminds me of giving and receiving love. They delighted in feeding us until we were well past full and even then they served us pie and dairy-free ice cream. While we picked up crumbs from the edges of our plates, I asked them what was the most important thing they learned since they met Tim, and in chorus they said, "Identity."

Regardless of whatever obstacle Tim faces or when he is tempted to believe lies more than truth, Tim knows and is firmly planted in his identity as a child of God—nothing more, nothing less. He did not preach to them or give them a study guide to follow, but with every trip to Whitey's ice cream or when they talked at church or got together to study Scripture, the thing Tim was overflowing with, his security in his identity in Christ, was constantly poured over them and prayed for them and it became part of who they are over time.

....

Shortly after I moved to Illinois, I was asked to speak at an event for teen girls a local church was hosting at a theater in Rock Island, one of the neighboring cities that make up the Quad Cities area. I didn't know, but I wouldn't actually be speaking that night. Tim arranged the fake event using a pastor he knew to book me to speak. There were tickets and posters and a Web site, so I never suspected a thing. I showed up to sound check an hour before the event began, but the theater was dark—not what you'd expect before an event.

That night, he proposed to me using that list of random things I had recited to him months before. A single rose waited for me at a table. Seven hundred and fifty balloons (no yellow) careened over the stage in the theater where he performed improv. Rubber ducks were everywhere. A magician came out and revealed two doves. A local high school marching band filed in and filled the theater with drumbeats and misplaced tuba notes. He proposed in a resting sea of colorful balloons, I said yes, and we walked outside where fireworks exploded over the roof of the theater as friends cheered.[1]

Since we were both married before, we opted to have a quiet wedding on a beach in Hawaii at sunrise and a huge party back home for everyone to celebrate with us. Rachel was there, and so were Kristoffer, James, and Wes. Friends who loved Tim during his darkest days now celebrated the new bright ones. Redemption and hope and love filled the room, soaking into the pores of everyone there. It was impossible not to see God.

Yes, there are the dusty ruins and dry bones of our stories that were interrupted by the actions of those who once promised to be true to us. We still mourn over the things that should have been, both for Tim and for me. And on occasion, we are reminded of them by people who do not know the full stories behind our previous marriages, who send anonymous messages to us wondering how long this marriage will last, and rejoicing over the brokenness of our divorces instead of mourning the loss of sacred covenants.

But we do not listen to those voices because those are not the voices of truth. Those who know us best and deeply know the details speak truth to us. And those people surround us as we walk forward, knowing the grace and redemption and second chance we both have been given, and they help us steward it and navigate it. The darkest part of my life has been given fresh breath and it may look like a happy ending with credits rolling and a fairy-tale movie fading to black. Yes, it is a redemption that is so good I can hardly believe I am not in a dream somewhere.

Because of both relationships and our careers, we decided to make a home for ourselves back in Nashville. Life has made a circle, or maybe it is a spiral. Either way, we have chosen to start our life in Nashville, committing for a year and keeping our eyes and hearts open for whatever story God wants us to write.

Before Tim and I moved to Nashville, I made a trip back to Holland to speak at a church and to catch up with friends. Christen and Tony were pregnant with their second child—a girl—and are moving to Turkey to be on the mission field. Christen and I sat at our accustomed table at Lemonjello's and I told her I put her letter in this book. We spoke as though no time had come between us and about how our relationship was special because the only expectation we had for each other was to simply be ourselves. We hugged one, then two, then three last times and I drove the familiar interstates back to Moline.

Tim and I spent a hurried and stressful week packing and saying good-bye to friends and family in Illinois. When we arrived at our new home in Franklin, new and old friends met us as we moved boxes from the truck into our new home, and moved pages in our books from one chapter into the next. Before pictures were hung or curtains were draped, before any of the boxes were broken down, familiar faces knocked on our door greeting us with hugs and food and invitations for dinner. The roots of our community started pulling us back into an embrace of safety and promise.

As we walk forward in our new lives as husband and wife, we know we cannot stop where we are and simply live in the glow. We know there are (and will be) hard times along our journey. And we know that the best way to prepare for surviving the bad and celebrating the good is to live in intentional, committed, and vulnerable community, together, with each other and with others and with God our Father, his Son, and the Holy Spirit.

The principle that we cannot give what we do not first receive works in reverse as we cannot receive what we do not give. We must spill the things that take root in us and we must place ourselves in a position to receive a refilling or we will run dry. It is a constant circle of pouring out and being poured into. We are all the woman at the well the moment after Jesus walked away and left her with life. Our source is never ending and we must run through the streets with joy exclaiming what is possible. Because of the way I was loved by my team and so many other friends, I can love. And because of the way they were loved by Christ, they could love me.

Father's Day arrived, and I sent Michael a note that said, "Even though you may not be my father, you've treated me like your daughter. Words are an inadequate way to say thank you, so know that I will forever carry the responsibility to love others the way you poured into me. I hope that I can repay you that way."

In some ways, this is practical and reasonable given the lessons life has taught Tim and me along the way. It is also really the only way we can say thank you to those who have wrapped us up in love as we learned those very lessons. We have the responsibility to respect and act on all we have been taught and to pass that on as best as we can to those we can.

14

BIG CHALLENGES AND
SMALL STEPS

The world is a fine place and worth fighting for.

—ERNEST HEMINGWAY

*W*riting on community is one of the most challenging things I've ever attempted. There are so many generalities yet so many specificities it's impossible for me to share them all in the pages of one small book. It's also impossible for the things in my story to apply to everybody's story.

Writing a *practical* book on community has been an even greater challenge. When my editors and I would talk about what this book should include and how it should be presented, we kept talking about the practical way my first book *Mad Church Disease: Overcoming the Burnout Epidemic* was written. There were four symptoms and five practical steps to take to stay healthy in ministry. I continue hearing now, six years after it was published, how easily it applied to people's lives.

As I started writing this book, it took on the pastoral voice of *Mad Church Disease*. But it didn't feel right. Four months into writing it, I deleted most of the manuscript and began again with a new outline that was equal parts narrative and application. It worked for a little while until I realized if I said one thing was the right thing to do, it was probably only applicable to a small percentage of the people reading my book. I can only hope that by discovering these recurring themes found in healthy community, somehow in some way someone somewhere can apply them to his or her own unique circumstances.

Then came the challenge of finding a story to illustrate certain ideas I wanted to talk about. What about boundaries in relationships? What about codependency? Margins? Should I use more Scripture? They're going to be mad there aren't more Bible verses in here and maybe even mad about the one time I drank whiskey and Coke in that old green recliner. I was halfway done with the book and sent it to a few people to read. Some wanted more theology and to know how to "do community better," and others asked if I was really writing what I wanted to write the way I felt like I was supposed to write it.

One of my favorite authors and a lovely friend, Josh Riebock, asked me, "Are you writing as boldly as you want? As unhinged as you want? I trust a hunch that may be totally inaccurate, but I think you're holding back. If that's true, or if it's not, either way—the eggshells you hear breaking when you write are only in your head. The greatest thing you can offer us is your courage."

His encouragement and challenge didn't stop there.

"Keep going. Let this book continue to evolve. Dig deeper. Feel more. Overthink less. Trust your instincts."

Overthink less? If anything, I felt I needed to think more. Is my story just a story? Or does it really point to the things about community that God used to redeem me when life looked over with and grey?

I have to believe it does. Let me rephrase.

I believe it does.

As I grow in my writing and in my beliefs on community, who I am as a child of Christ and the message he has given me to share with you, I must rely only on what he has pressed into my heart like a wax seal that cannot be broken without being damaged.

I am comforted in the idea that Jesus rarely instructed without parable. Truth is communicated through stories; they are principles that wear flesh and breathe air and feel pain and joy. Recalling a quote from Madeleine L'Engle, "Jesus was not a theologian. He was God who told stories."[1]

As people learned I was writing a book on themes of intimacy within Christian community, over and over again I heard the question, "Have you read Dietrich Bonhoeffer's book on community?" Ages ago, I skimmed it over at a bookstore, but for whatever insane reason didn't purchase it. In the middle of writing this book, I bought a copy of *Life Together* and spent an afternoon with lots of coffee poring over his timeless words and thoughts on what "community" is and should look like in the church.

I am passionate about relationships. Were it not for intentional, sacrificial, gracious, difficult, truth-speaking relationships, my feet would have wandered far off the path where I believe God has placed me. Originally, this book wasn't going to have an explanation, other than the narrative itself. Diving in headfirst was the plan, but after reading *Life Together*, I knew I had to better define this attempt to communicate such a large message in a small package. People who like very practical things and how-to guides and instructions for living in better community may be frustrated at this memoir. There's a section of study guides and reflections in the back for those who like to take a practical approach to implementing these ideas.

What I ask you to recognize now is that the ability to even be in relationship with others is a gift and a privilege. We think it is a right, an entitlement. Maybe even a calling. On a most basic level of understanding, yes: we are called to have relationships with others. However, the basis of these relationships is formed in our commonality, which is Christ. Through him and by him are relationships even viable. Bonhoeffer affirms,

> Christianity means community through Jesus Christ and in Jesus Christ. No Christian community is more or less than this. Whether it be a brief, single encounter or a daily fellowship of years, Christian community is only this. We belong to one another only through and in Jesus Christ.[2]

So that we may not hold the ideal of community higher than the one who provides it through his Son, as we seek to better understand relational dynamics and pursue holy, healthy interactions, we must remain rooted first and foremost in our identity that is found in being a son or daughter of our God. It is from this core truth that our relationships originate and flourish. But we must not put the ideal first or our relationships will eventually fall incredibly short of the divine purpose God intended. Bonheoffer continues,

> He who loves his dream of a community more than the Christian community itself becomes a destroyer of the latter, even though his personal intentions may be ever so honest and earnest and sacrificial . . . We are bound together by faith, not by experience . . . Through him alone do we have access to one another, joy in one another, and fellowship with one another.[3]

We must look ever so deeply into the desire we feel to connect with others and recognize that it is more than what it seems; it is the Holy Spirit within us acknowledging the Holy Spirit within another. There is both heaviness and joy that come with the responsibility of recognizing the obligation and gift to participate within this kingdom on earth. How can we purposefully and mindfully pursue these relationships?

God has implanted this passion for holy relationships profoundly and enigmatically into who I am. Simply stated, this book shares how God is redeeming my story and how he has given me hope through my relationship with him. Sometimes, my relationship with him felt empty. God appeared silent. It was only over the course of time that I recognized the hope he was giving me was often expressed through my relationship with others, spirit to spirit.

Yet while this passion to be in, to create, to nourish, and to explore these intentional, vulnerable, committed relationships flares through my veins, at the same time, I face a resistance. We all do, I think.

There is a wedding Tim and I were invited to, and I've been looking forward to it all week, imagining what I'll wear and what songs they'll play and if there are going to be gluten-free options at the reception and what friends I'll see. But the wedding is two hours from the time that I am writing this, and I dread going. I am tired from writing and keeping my house clean and I am so far behind on my e-mails and office work it's horrific. I just want to sit and stare at a wall and not see or talk to anyone. Traci, who I mentioned earlier, works next door to the coffee shop I often write from and she knew how I was diving into this book and that I also really like to be left alone when I'm in this "zone." So that she wouldn't bother me while I worked, she so sweetly invited me over for dinner (via text) with her family last night. I wanted to go. I love her, her husband is funny, and her kids are adorable. Did I go? No. Tim was out of town and I was feeling sorry for myself. I should have engaged in community but I chose not to. I finished a good day of writing, drove home, sat on my couch, and ate peanut butter from the jar and drank a glass of red wine and watched *Dateline* and sent her an apology text. *An apology text.* There are unanswered text messages in my phone about getting lunch or going out with several friends, but I do not reply because there is still something in me that wants to stay tucked away, isolated, alone. There is a selfishness and I have not completely mastered overcoming it in spite of my very best attempts and the lessons I've learned . . . and now written about in this book. I practice what I preach so well in my heart, but when it comes to actually living it out consistently in my life, I have the tendency to be just as selfish, just as closed off (and, as a result), just as lonely. To make a bold confession, sometimes I like living in this dark space. Sometimes I do. It is familiar and is not scary. At least that's what I believe, yet at the same time, know it to not be true.

I still fear rejection, condemnation, abandonment, losing someone, betrayal, being intimate, change. I fear the vulnerability. I am too lazy or sometimes the opposite, too overworked and overly committed to the unimportant to actually commit to relationships in the way I've experienced in the past and the way I desire to do now. Will I be enough? What if I do the wrong thing? What if they don't love me? What if I don't love them?

We will always feel a complex, two-sided longing—the craving for relationships and the desire to be on our own—creep in as we pull our feet through the mud of the daily. When this comes, we must take a heavy breath and command our spirits to rejoice and reach out. If we are told a rock will sing when we don't, imagine the will it takes to get a defeated soul to move. Command it anyway. Rejoice anyway. We are children of the One who has loved us in the past for eons and will love us into forever for eternity. A Man died in our place, painting us pure and lovely, and nothing can steal this away from us. Not even our own selfishness.

It is in moments of brief grace and clear thinking when I realize there isn't one moment when it's right enough or when we're ready enough to love. There are times when we are depleted and we need to be poured into, but even in those moments we can look around for the small ways to show love: opening a door for someone, tipping the waiter just a little more, or sending a small note to a friend letting them know you're thinking about them. These small moments carry great weight, maybe even more than being available for the bigger moments in life (though those special times are certainly important too!).

Start small, be faithful, and see what God will do when you are intentional, vulnerable, and committed to consistently living and loving and serving in relationships with others.

RESOURCES

*I*n writing *Lean on Me*, it's my desire to show you that whatever course you find yourself on, you are not alone, you need God, and you need others. This book (or any other for that matter) cannot tell you what to do to find a perfect community (spoiler: it doesn't exist here on earth). No book can give you a guide that lists out steps on how you should structure the people and events in your life in order for you to feel complete. It can't be done. Instead, I pray that you will see God's hand at work in my beautifully broken and gracefully redeemed life and know that the same healing from him is available for you too. And through being intentional, vulnerable, and committed in relationships with other believers, your life will not be one of easiness or perfection, but it will be one of light and love and hope.

Because there are so many relational nuances this book was not able to cover, I thought I'd point you to some resources I've found helpful along the way that are more specific to certain dynamics within relationships:

Henry Cloud and John Townsend. *Boundaries: When to Say Yes, When to Say No, to Take Control of Your Life*. Rev. ed. Grand Rapids: Zondervan, 1992.

Larry Crab. *Connecting: Healing Ourselves and Our Relationships*. Nashville: Thomas Nelson, 2004.

Melody Beattie. *Codependent No More: How to Stop Controlling Others and Start Caring for Yourself*. Center City, MN: Hazelden, 1986.

Brené Brown. *The Gifts of Imperfection: Let Go of Who You Think You're Supposed to Be and Embrace Who You Are*. Center City, MN: Hazelden, 2010.

Henry Cloud and John Townsend. *Safe People: How to Find Relationships That Are Good for You and Avoid Those That Aren't*. Grand Rapids: Zondervan, 1996.

Henry Cloud. *Necessary Endings: The Employees, Businesses, and Relationships That All of Us Have to Give Up in Order to Move Forward*. New York: HarperBusiness, 2011.

M. Scott Peck. *The Road Less Traveled, Timeless Edition: A New Psychology of Love, Traditional Values and Spiritual Growth*. New York: Touchstone, 2003.

Henri Nouwen. *The Wounded Healer: Ministry in Contemporary Society*. Colorado Springs: Image Books, 1979.

Richard Rohr. *Immortal Diamond: The Search for Our True Self*. San Francisco: Jossey-Bass, 2013.

Richard Rohr. *Everything Belongs: The Gift of Contemplative Prayer*. New York: The Crossroad Publishing Company, 2003.

Dietrich Bonhoeffer. *Life Together: The Classic Exploration of Faith in Community.* New York: HarperOne, 2009.

Charles Colson. *Being the Body.* Nashville: Thomas Nelson, 2004.

James Wilhoit and Dallas Willard. *Spiritual Formation as if the Church Mattered: Growing in Christ through Community.* Grand Rapids: Baker Academic, 2008.

ACKNOWLEDGMENTS

*F*ather and Savior, thank you for trusting me with pain, silence, and joy.

Tim Miller, my best friend, my husband. You are the most passionate and compassionate person I know. I'm so glad you wrote me awkward messages in the sand.

There are infinite numbers of people I need to say thank you to. Though some of you are in the manuscript (please consider that my thanks!), some of you are not.

At the risk of leaving people out, I will attempt to remember as many as possible. Steve and Jude, McSweeney, Liz, Ed, Daniel, Eve and Charlie, Monte, Kyle and Holiday, LV, Audrey, Charlie, Sonja, Bob and Maria, Luis, Christopher, Michael, Susan and Larry, Don, Lindsey, Kym, Brian, Adam, Tim H., Crystal, Kate, Joel and Kathy, Christen and Tony, Adam and Jenna, Brooke, Lemonjello's, Brandon, Angela, Adam, Art and Christy, Beth, Barry and Lori, Bryon, Amber, Burt and Careen, Jed, Trent, Josh and Jenny, Carly, Chad, Christy, DVO, Drew, Eli and Shawna,

Nate, Hannah, Jamie, Jessica, Jenn, Jeremy, Jim and Solveig, Karl, Lane, Chad and Lynse, Adam and Marko, Ward, MPJ, Sarah, Spence, Susanna, Tara, Theresa, Jim and Melissa, St. B's, Passion Church, Quad Cities Prayer Center, Ben and Paige, Patrick, Nate and Kat, Connect Coffee House, Steve and Amber, Matt and Traci, J, the Other J, Tara, Caleb, Elena, Matt and Rose, James, Kristoffer, Wesley, Christina, Austin and Katy, Seth and Hannah, Heather, Aaron, Jeff, Josh, Ian, Tara Brown, Joshua, Justin and Andrea, Adam and Anna, Lexie, BriBiz, Lysa, Phil and Tasha, the Millers (all of you!), the Linebargers, and _____. Because I know I forgot you. Please write your name in and forgive me.

Thank you to Matt and my entire team at Thomas Nelson.

Thank you to everyone who supported me on Kickstarter and supported poetry:

Karen!!, Lori Ventola, Thomas Bingaman, Christopher Marshburn, Andrew Stewart, Tamera Bryan, Elizabeth Harshaw, Stacy Wood, Jennifer Morel, Amanda Mae Arnold, Anonymous, Matthew Litchfield, Paul OBriant, Natalie Barton, Debra S., Valerie McGowan, Meeshee Scherrei, Octavio Cesar Martinez, @holycowcreative, Crystal Renaud, Pamela E. Crane, Guy Delcambre, Indy Snow, Darlene Hotaling, Karin Haubold, Audrey Price, Linda Matlack, Shannon Douglas, Natalie Burris, Mona Hanna, Daphne, Chad Burrus, Jonathan, Annie Bethancourt, Lisa Spagnolo, Jennifer Barrett, Aaron Smith, Melissa Martin, Michael Raburn, Albert, Scott Sapp, John R. Wallace, Benjamin D. Christensen, Jason, Rick Smith, Jeremiah Meeks BSHD, Julie Adams—New Zealand, Katy Moynihan, Blaine Hogan, David Stone, joeybeatrix, Gail Mayes, Joe Sewell, Santos and Amanda

Samayoa, Connie Shuler Barlow, Katie Ullmann, Julie B., Justin Schmitt, Amber Elstad, Andrew W. Montoya, Jen Rose, Justin Falls, Micah Ogle, Jo Hilder, Josh Oxley, Lisa Pippus, Paul Stackhouse, Sam Mahlstadt, Pat, Amanda Faith Moore, Scott Elliott, @chadjarnagin, Sonny Lemmons, Lisa Jane Mcauley, Nate Ragan, Naomi, Amy Bennett, Jeffrey Campbell, Shawn, Terrace Crawford, Solveig Leithaug, Ione Flanagan, the Niebuhrs, Bob Bond, Matthew Ryan Wood, Carrie Davis Ben-Ezra, Larry Shallenberger, Amanda Johnson, Miriam Ruth, Faunty, Carol Asher, Matthew K. Wiley, Anita Mathias, Travis, Joanna Holman, Mark Cole, Patrick Dodd, Stephen Hurn, Carolyn Evaine Counterman, Nate Macy, Misty M., Rhiannon Parks, Kaira Butler, Andrew Yang, Theresa Johnson, Dedra and Mike Herod, John Murphy, Phyllis Tsang, Mike and Shelia Mullican, Desirae Schneider, Tim Jones, Stacy Aannestad, Kyle Newcomb, Jackey Chapman, E. T. Mair, Joe Kennedy, Amy Maltrud, Candi Deal, Melissa Culbreth, Jesse, Kelsey Wynns, Brynn Morris, Rachel Anne Jackson, Steve Burrow, Jordan Balint, Tony McCollum, Sheryl Root, Doug Hart, Ally, Dawn M. Underwood, Kim Kuzmkowski, Trina Lee, Ashley and Aaron Linne, Steve Gilbert, Jaymie-Lyn, Jared Fehrenbach, Aaron Matthews, Michael H. Smith, Yvette E. Johnson-Brabant, Tom Davis, John T. Williams, Dena Griswold, Dan and Erin Lacher, Tim and Jenny Morrison, the Chambers Family Villagers, Aaron "Big Smooth" Hines, M. E. Becker, David and Rhonda Kemp, Jim Watters, Lauree Ashcom, J. D. R., Scott and Viktoria Harrison, Phil Makower, Rev. Terry Webster, Tom, Billy Ritchie, Kelly J. Black—Wired for Joy!, Pat Mulvihill, Michael Evanchak, Bruce and Heather Moore.

Reader's Guide

1

CREATED FOR BELONGING

Reflections

1. Have you ever experienced the feeling of "needing to belong"? What about the opposite feeling of desiring to be independent from others?
2. What was your childhood like? Did you move around or stay in one place? Did you ever feel that you had a home where you lived?
3. Do situations in your past—positive or negative—affect your ability and desire to trust others now? Which ones?
4. What has your experience been like with small groups in churches? Do you feel as if you can be vulnerable and committed or does a part of you hold back? What fears do you have about being vulnerable, if any?
5. In John 13:35, Jesus tells us the world will know we are his disciples and his followers by the love we have for

each other. What is one way you have seen believers show love that has given you joy?

Next Right Step

We are all created to belong in community by being there for others and asking for help when we need it. Sometimes fears and hang-ups can prevent us from choosing to acknowledge and act. Can you make a choice to accept our need for others and to be willing to love and serve others without hesitation?

Prayer

Lord Jesus, I know you have designed us to be in relationship with you and with others. Please help me fight any fears I face and open up the doors to community so that not only can I be in healthy relationships and find a place to belong, but that also the world can see that I love and follow you.

2

WHERE ARE YOU?

Reflections

1. When Adam and Eve sinned, fear and shame entered the world for the first time. Do you think fear and shame play a role in our relationships with each other? What about our relationship with God?

2. God desires for us to be in relationship with him. When he asks, "Where are you?" what is your answer? Tell him where you are—near to him? Far from him? Be honest. He is pursuing you.

3. If you had to plot yourself on a graph, where would you be in the areas of vulnerability and commitment with your key relationships in life? Your spouse? Your family? Your closest friends? Your acquaintances? Are you living both vulnerably and committed in appropriate relationships?

"VULNERABILITY"	Not Vulnerable and Not Committed	Committed and Not Vulnerable
	Vulnerable and Not Committed	Committed and Vulnerable

"COMMITMENT"

4. Have you ever experienced a conflict in a relationship that ended the relationship? What about a conflict that caused the relationship to grow?

Next Right Step

What are some actions you can take to develop healthier relationships by becoming more vulnerable and committed? Think of people you know you can trust but maybe haven't opened up to. Are there people who need to know you are there for them? Is there a conflict that has not yet been resolved that is preventing you from growing in your relationships?

Prayer

Lord Jesus, please help me see people through the eyes you see them with. Give me courage to open up and share where I need help and give me love and grace to show when others need me to help them. If there is conflict in my life and in my relationships, please make it known to me and give me wisdom on how to solve it so that nothing comes between you, me, and my relationships with others.

3

RELATING IN THE EVERYDAY AND THE CRISIS

Reflections

1. Do you ever feel that people are only there for the crisis and it's often difficult to connect in the everyday? Or vice versa?

2. Sociologists have been researching the increasing sense of loneliness in the modern Western world and have concluded that the increase in technology, wealth, and materialism have led to this. Would you agree with their findings? What is your experience as things have changed in your life over time?

3. Does the feeling of being overwhelmed affect your ability to connect with others?

4. Have you experienced a crisis in your life that has shown

you how strong or weak your community is? What was it? How did people respond?

Next Right Step

Relationships are important in the everyday and the crisis. Being available in the everyday helps us to be ready to serve in a crisis, and showing up for someone's crisis moment allows us freedom to speak into their everyday moments. In the same way, we need to allow others to participate in our mundane and our emergencies. Can you think of a way to show someone that you are "just there" for them? Invite someone over for a meal or offer to plan a play date. Do you know of anyone experiencing a crisis? Contact them and let them know you are praying for them and offer to help in some specific way . . . and follow through.

Prayer

Lord Jesus, please help me to see that you are the Creator of time and space, and everything you have given me is yours. This includes my schedule, my relationships, and my resources. Please help me see where I can show others love daily and through hard times, and please help me to receive love from others when they try to invest into my life relationally.

4

CHOOSING THE SHELTER
OF RELATIONSHIPS

Reflections

1. Have you ever "run away" from something? Maybe you moved to escape or left a conflict or changed a job because it seemed easier to leave than to stay. Was it a good decision? A bad one? Why?
2. When we are living outside of God's plan for us, away from people and accountability, we often feel the effects of it in many ways: emotionally, spiritually, and physically. Can you recall a time in your life when you experienced this?
3. My friend Liz confronted me on my poor decision to move from Nashville to California. Do you have a friend in your life whom you are willing to listen to when he or she challenges you with difficult things?

4. Do you think relationships should only occur organically? Or do you think they sometimes need intentionality to begin?
5. I told myself "real relationships only happen out of thin air." What are some of the messages you tell yourself about relationships that may be colored by your perception of the past?

Next Right Step

If you haven't already, evaluate where you are in your relationships with others. Are there any you need to become either more vulnerable or more committed to? Commit to taking a step of intentionality in growing those relationships. Can you ask a friend or a group of friends to make a time commitment to intentionally growing your relationships with each other and make a list of things in which you can help each other grow?

Prayer

Lord Jesus, I thank you for the gift of relationships and for giving me a desire to belong. Please help me find the time and courage to approach people in my life and invite them into genuine, consistent, and growing relationships.

FALLING INTO SURRENDER

Reflections

1. Sadly, many people in the church have been abused or taken advantage of when they have submitted themselves to other people's authority. Because of these painful experiences, the idea of surrendering or submitting to others in relationships is frightening and can be met with a tremendous amount of resistance. Do you find yourself hesitant when it comes to the idea of inviting another person into your life in such an intimate and vulnerable way?

2. In regard to the word *community* in the church, some people have had a negative experience with small groups. Others had a negative experience in a less-structured environment. As a result, both camps of people speak unenthusiastically about how the church—however it is

defined in their mind—has failed. People outside of the faith see the disunity this causes. Do you fall into one camp? Which one? Is there anything you can change in your approach that unifies the body?

3. Surrender first begins with our surrender to God. It's difficult to let go of the expectations and selfishness we place in our lives and trust him completely with our identity and outcomes. Do you find surrendering to God easy or difficult to do?

4. When we surrender to others, we surrender our need to be right and to be heard. We serve and keep a quiet spirit. We risk being hurt by someone who doesn't approach relationships in the same manner. While we do need to be wise about who we are vulnerable with, we can't let fear keep us out of relationships. Where do you see more potential to have honest relationships? Or the potential to be hurt?

5. Brené Brown has studied vulnerability and connection in relationships and has concluded it is our imperfections that keep us from relationships; that showing our flaws makes us unworthy. Have you ever felt the need to "have it all together" in order to be loved and accepted in a relationship?

Next Right Step

Identify whether surrender is difficult or easy for you and know it's often different for everyone depending on past situations and present relationships. If surrendering in relationships is difficult, what moments in your past have caused you to build up walls? List them, and if there are any people you need to forgive, work through that with a friend, counselor, or pastor. These are likely deep wounds. If surrender comes easy, though it may sound counterintuitive, make sure those you are asking to be a close part of your life are ready for the responsibility. Nobody is ever "perfect" or "ready," but it's important for you and the other person to know the level of commitment and responsibility surrender carries.

Prayer

Lord Jesus, please help me see my need for others. Show me where I have been hurt in the past and where I have built up walls that may keep me from trusting you and others. Proverbs 4:23 says to "guard your heart." Help me protect my heart by trusting it to you, not to my own will and hands. Please guide me into relationships that are healthy and ready to both "lean on" and "be leaned on" as we walk forward for your glory.

6

THE IMPORTANCE OF DIVERSITY

Reflections

1. Have you ever had a close relationship with someone who was totally different than you in age, stage of life, faith, ethnicity, racial background, or political views? What did you notice about the relationship? Did you learn things you may not have learned otherwise?

2. When close relationships are diverse, not only do you have the chance to learn from other perspectives, but by default, you begin acquiring the qualities of those you spend time with. What are some characteristics you'd like to see improved in your life?

3. When Jesus chose his disciples, they became more like him. Becoming more Christlike should be something all believers strive toward. Think of the fruit of the

Spirit listed in Galatians 5: Love, joy, peace, patience, kindness, goodness, faithfulness, gentleness, and self-control. Which of these characteristics can you focus on incorporating into your daily life?

4. Sometimes geography can separate a close friendship. Do you have close friends whom you frequently stay in contact with who live far away? How do you manage those relationships?

Next Right Step

Is your community fairly monotone? Is everyone the same age or in the same life stage? Consider asking someone older and someone younger or someone with a different background to your close group of friends.

Prayer

Lord Jesus, thank you for the diversity you give us in the Church. I pray you open my eyes to see the uniqueness that each story brings. Is there someone you'd like for me to reach out to and learn from? Is there someone you'd like for me to reach out to and teach? Please show me how to best embrace the diversity around me to show the world the beauty that is in your kingdom.

7

LOSING CONTROL AND
EMBRACING COMMITMENT

Reflections

1. In chapter 5, examining our ability to surrender was likely a difficult task. Commitment goes one step beyond surrender. It's important to note the difference. *"Commitment, at its root, is the idea of sending a pledge of faith into the future."* In your own words, how would you define the difference between surrender and commitment?

2. Have you ever heard the phrase *committed to Christ*? When you commit your life to Christ, you believe God's Son, Jesus, came to this earth and died for our sins and was raised again and that we receive the Holy Spirit as a mediator. Once we believe, the Bible assures us that

we are saved and will spend eternity with him. Daily we must lay down our own wills and lives and pledge to seek and follow him, trusting him *fully*. Do you daily commit your life to him?

3. It is scary to fully commit and surrender to a group of people. By committing to them, you don't become their "puppet," by which you must do and say everything they ask. Instead, you are submitting to them so that both you and the community can become more like Christ—not to have a power trip. *This is probably one of the most difficult decisions you can make.* What hesitations do you have, if any, about submitting yourself to a group of people?

4. In addition to submitting yourself to a community, you can commit specific things for them to help you be accountable with. For me, getting healthy physically, emotionally, spiritually, and relationally, as well as being responsible with my finances, were all things I submitted to them. If I was making a decision that fell into one of these categories, I would ask them for their counsel, and with God's help and guidance, make a decision. What are some areas in your life that you could submit to others to help you grow?

Next Right Step

It may feel like a daunting task, but committing yourself and specific aspects of your life into community is a wise and vulnerable thing to do. When our relationships are uncomfortable because we are being challenged and growing, it's a good thing. Pray and talk to someone you consider to be wise about what it looks like for you to intentionally submit yourself to serving a community and allowing them to speak into your life.

Prayer

Lord Jesus, being committed in community is so hard. I want to stay in control of my own life, the things I do, and how I live. Please help me to surrender my will to you, and to submit and commit my life to your Church. Please help me to see the kingdom benefits that occur when believers are mutually and lovingly submitted to each other.

PRACTICING VULNERABILITY

Reflections

1. Have you ever experienced a season in life when you felt completely alone? Did it seem as though God was not listening and that if you brought your worries to others you would only be burdening them? Describe how you felt and the choices you made.

2. After making a bad decision or struggling with something you were ashamed of, did you ever make the choice to confess and open up to someone even though you were afraid? If you did, how did you feel after? If you didn't, what kept you from being vulnerable?

3. Sometimes it seems easier to open up to someone you don't know rather than someone you do. When I was in Lincoln, Illinois, and had my "fight" with God, I felt the need to confess and chose a church where I didn't know

anyone. Though this was a good first step—speaking the words out loud to another person—I still needed someone who knew me well to follow up with me and ask how I was doing. Do you find it easier to open up to strangers or to those who are close to you?

4. Do you believe this statement is true: "It is a paradox: once we realize being vulnerable is never safe, we are then free to be vulnerable"? Why or why not?

Next Right Step

Is something in your life weighing down your spirit that you need to confess to another person? James 5:16 (NLT) says, *"Confess your sins to each other and pray for each other so that you may be healed. The earnest prayer of a righteous person has great power and produces wonderful results."* The word "healed" in the passage indicates a weight that has been bound and lifted from one's spirit or a spiritual healing. Galatians 6:2 (NLT) says, *"Share each other's burdens, and in this way obey the law of Christ."* Can you share your burden with another so they can help you carry it? Can you make yourself available for another person so they can lean on you?

Prayer

Lord Jesus, thank you for the gift of your guidance through Scripture. You show us how by confessing the things that weigh us down, we can experience freedom and healing. You also instruct us to carry each other's burdens. Please reveal to me anything I should confess so that I may be free from its weight. Also, please show me if I can step into someone's life and be a person who helps them carry their weight for a season.

9

PERSEVERING THROUGH PAIN

Reflections

1. In your life, have you experienced a season of good followed by a season of bad? Did the discouragement cause you to want to give up?

2. When times are tough, it's easy to escape. For some, abusing TV, social media, food, or alcohol may be a coping mechanism. Is there one habit you immediately crave or pursue when you feel stuck or disheartened?

3. Read Paul's struggle in Romans 7:14–25. Have you ever felt the confusion he talks about in this passage? Do you experience the war between wanting to do right but feeling as though you can't?

4. In our modern world, we can almost get anything we want instantly. When I visited Susan's church, I learned

the phrase "the slow and inefficient work of God." Can you look back on your life and see the things God has done in your life that took time—often a lot of time?

5. In order to persevere, we need others to remind us of God's love and to encourage us to stay in the fight when we want to give up. What are some ways you have been encouraged by friends during difficult times?

Next Right Step

Chances are, either you or someone you know is experiencing a difficult time right now. It's hard to have hope and stay focused on being in community. If you are the one who needs some support, reach out to a friend and ask. Share what you're going through and if you feel the need to escape somehow. If you're in a peaceful season, take a look around and see who may be going through something tough. Reach out to them and let them know they are loved and offer your support in a specific way.

Prayer

Lord Jesus, it can be so difficult to persevere when seasons of life seem hopeless. Sometimes, I admit, even you feel far away. Please help me to see all the ways you are near me. Give me wisdom when I need to reach out for help or when I need to be there for someone else. Show me the best way I can love and help me to be humble so I can receive love.

10

THE COLLISION OF FAITH AND HOPE

Reflections

1. Have you ever had an encounter with God that was unexpected, like the time I was driving home with the tacky Christmas tree?
2. There is no magic formula for getting through a hard season, even when you engage with your community as much as possible. God often gives us seasons of silence and waiting as well as seasons of joy and abundance. What are some practical ways you can remind yourself, and others, that God is faithful even during the times we wait?
3. After we have spent time learning and growing in community, it becomes easier to ask for advice and trust in the decisions the group has made. When I thought going back to school was a good idea, I bounced the idea

off my team and they gave me full support. Have you
ever experienced the confidence that comes with having
a decision affirmed?

4. In addition to having decisions come easier after
spending time in community, we recognize the elements
that make a group of people healthy: intentionality,
vulnerability, and consistency. When I moved to
Holland, Michigan, to return to school, I applied these
principles to my new friendships, and very quickly a rich
and healthy community formed. What do you think
makes this type of community possible?

Next Right Step

We can't always plan when we'll encounter a moment of indescribable joy, or when we'll shift from a dark season to one full
of light. In both, we need others so we can be reminded of God's
faithfulness or so that we can share our joy and hope when others need to hear it. Where are you? Are you in a season of joy or a
season of pain (or maybe a season somewhere in between)? Can
you reach out to someone if you need a reminder of God's faithfulness? Or can you share your story of how God came through
to encourage a friend?

Prayer

Lord Jesus, I am grateful that you promise to never leave us or
forsake us. Especially during seasons of trial, this can be hard to

remember. Please remind me, when I am weary, of the joy that you promise us. And when I have a story of your hope to pass along to someone else, please embed that into my heart so it cannot escape!

....
11
....

RECEIVING AND RETURNING

Reflections

1. Darrell Vesterfelt said, "We can't give gifts we haven't received first." What does this statement mean to you in light of community and sharing in the joy we, as believers, find in Christ?

2. Sometimes we don't believe small actions mean much, but sometimes they're what matters most. Recall a time in your life when someone did something that seemed small but made a huge difference.

3. It's easy to compare what we have (or don't have) to someone else. Maybe you can't invite a person to live with you for several months while they get back on their feet, or you can't write a check to someone who needs some financial assistance, but there is always something we can do to help someone. When we pair up with others

in our community, we can have an even greater impact. What is something you *can* contribute to help your community and someone in need?

Next Right Step

If you're in a committed and vulnerable community, get together with those you can. Have each person offer what he or she can to help someone in need. Maybe it's a place to stay, a meal, a job connection, or company. Is there anyone within your community who needs help?

If you're not in a group yet, offer what you can to someone who needs it. Your action may be the beginning of finding community!

Prayer

Lord Jesus, thank you for always providing for us. So often we take for granted what we have when we compare our lives with others. Please show me how I can best love those in my community as well as those who may be strangers by being generous with what you have given me.

12

SAFE PLACES

Reflections

1. Inviting others into our lives can be scary. With the dating, marriage, and parenting trends changing so quickly, we often think we're better off when we handle our personal business on our own. Because of mistakes I made when I was newly single, I learned the value of seeking advice from my community so I wouldn't make the same mistakes again. Would you consider asking for counsel from others even in the most private matters in your life?

2. Even though I only lived in Holland, Michigan, a little over a year, I was able to establish a solid community and a couple of close, lifelong friends. Have you ever experienced a friendship that developed quickly and deeply?

3. Moving into a new city is a huge (and stressful) transition, even when we may be acquainted with a few people. What steps can you take to engage with and establish friendships if you're in a season of life that's new and unfamiliar?

Next Right Step

Are you facing a decision about marriage or parenting? Or are you in the middle of another type of transition, whether it be work-related, moving, or in your family? Invite someone in to help you make the best decisions possible.

Prayer

Lord Jesus, in you we always find safety and we know that you always have our best interests in mind. As we encounter transition in our lives, please give us the proactive attitude to ask for wisdom along the way. May we also make ourselves available to help those around us in any transition they face.

13

CIRCLES OR SPIRALS

Reflections

1. Titus 2:1–8 (NLT) says:

As for you, Titus, promote the kind of living that reflects wholesome teaching. Teach the older men to exercise self-control, to be worthy of respect, and to live wisely. They must have sound faith and be filled with love and patience.

Similarly, teach the older women to live in a way that honors God. They must not slander others or be heavy drinkers. Instead, they should teach others what is good. These older women must train the younger women to love their husbands and their children, to live wisely and be pure, to work in their homes, to do good, and to be submissive to their husbands. Then they will not bring shame on the word of God.

In the same way, encourage the young men to live wisely. And you yourself must be an example to them by doing good works of every kind. Let everything you do reflect the integrity and seriousness of your teaching. Teach the truth so that your teaching can't be criticized.

This is a rich example of how discipleship and mentoring fit in with community. Although Rachel, the young girl I mentor, and Kristoffer, James, and Wes, the young men Tim mentored, were not in our "core" community, we recognized the need to share with others who are younger than us the things we have learned in community and from those who are older than us. Families are becoming more disjointed and the media influences most social activities. Do you see a need for those living in healthy community to disciple (to teach to be more like Jesus) and mentor younger men and women?

2. Does your church or an organization in your community offer mentoring? What would it look like if you and a friend signed up for the next year?

3. Have you considered asking someone to mentor you? What happened?

Next Right Step

Regardless of how new you are to the Christian faith or how long you've been in community with others, you can always share your experiences with those who are in younger generations. Look for ways that you can follow Paul's instruction to always "teach the truth."

Prayer

Lord Jesus, thank you for giving me the experiences I've had in my life. Although there are some I may regret and am not proud of, you promise you will use them for good. Please help me steward both the good and the bad chapters of my life so that others can learn from them and grow to know you.

14

BIG CHALLENGES AND SMALL STEPS

Reflections

1. Relationships, community, discipleship . . . these are all large topics with large theological and practical implications. Dietrich Bonhoeffer wrote that we are given community only through Christ when he said, "We belong to one another only through and in Jesus Christ." What do you think of his statement?

2. It can be easy to put a greater importance on "finding community" than growing in our relationship with Christ. Community is important, but unless we are consistently spending time with our Father God, it will never reach the potential he has planned for it. What are some ways you can practically and consistently fellowship with Christ?

3. Even those most passionate about genuine community

(like myself) struggle with the duality of forces mentioned throughout this book: the need to belong and the need to be independent. Can you make a commitment to yourself and to someone else that even in the times you feel like withdrawing or isolating, you'll reach out and let one other person know what you're feeling?

Next Right Step

Identify those you consider to be at the core of your community. Can you make a covenant with each other to be intentional, vulnerable, and committed to each other consistently, knowing you'll face seasons of conflict and joy? Start by making a commitment for six months or a year, and see what God does to shape you and those around you!

Prayer

Lord Jesus, I am grateful that you have brought me to a place in life where I desire to be with others and to be known by others. Please increase my love for you and for the people you place in my life. It is only through Jesus that we are able to have this kind of fellowship, the kind of fellowship that can have a great impact for your kingdom and glory. I pray my actions and relationships bring you just that—glory to your name.

NOTES

Chapter 2
1. Genesis 3:8.
2. 1 John 1:9.

Chapter 4
1. Anne Jackson, *Permission to Speak Freely* (Nashville: Thomas Nelson, 2010), 177. With a special thanks to my friend Jamie Tworkowski for pointing this truth out.

Chapter 5
1. My grandfather's last words, "Never give up on church," were written as a dedication to him in my first book, *Mad Church Disease: Overcoming the Burnout Epidemic.* Were it not for these words, I probably would be living my life very far outside of God's will. Thanks again, Grandpa.
2. I was using Matthew 18:20 out of context.
3. Dr. Brené Brown, TED Talk, June 2010, http://www.ted.com/talks/ brene_brown_on_vulnerability.
4. Isaiah 26:3.

Chapter 8
1. Vulnerable. Dictionary.com. Unabridged. Random House, Inc., http://dictionary.reference.com/browse/vulnerable (accessed: March 4, 2014).

Chapter 9
1. Romans 5:3–4.

Chapter 10
1. "We Are" by the Album Leaf was playing as I was writing this, and it simply captivated me how similar these lyrics are to what I was writing.

Chapter 11
1. 1 John 4:19.
2. John 13:8 The Voice.
3. Allison Vesterfelt, "A Surprising Way to Become More Generous," Storyline. June 13, 2013. Accessed September 23, 2013. http://storylineblog. com/2013/06/13/a-surprising-way-to-become-more-generous.
4. John 13:9 The Voice.

Chapter 12
1. "Night Must End" by Sleeping at Last.

Chapter 13
1. You can see Tim's proposal at http://www.timandannemiller.com and reading the About Us page.

Chapter 14
1. Madeline L'Engle, *Walking on Water: Reflections on Faith and Art* (New York: North Point Press, 1980), 54.
2. Dietrich Bonhoeffer, *Life Together* (New York: Harper & Row, 1954), 21.
3. Ibid., 27.